Contents

Introduction

The word *kingdom* is an important word in the Bible. This is evident by its frequent usage by Jesus in the Gospels. Since the kingdom of God, the kingdom of heaven, and the everlasting kingdom are for the children of God, they should be acquainted with what the Bible teaches about the subject.

The books studied in this manual—1 and 2 Samuel—record the history of the beginnings of the kingdom era of Israel, including the kingdom of David, a type of Christ's kingdom. May this study guide help you see the highlights of that era and their significance in the total plan of God. Beyond that, may you learn valuable spiritual lessons for your own Christian experience.

Incorporated in this self-study guide are various helps on analyzing the Bible chapter by chapter and paragraph by paragraph. Convinced that "the pencil is one of the best eyes," the writer has also given suggestions along the way on how the student may record this analysis on paper.

These lessons may be used either for individual or group Bible study. When several are studying together it would be well to have a leader.

The leader should observe the following suggestions:

1. If any lesson seems too long for one meeting, use half the assigned work and leave the other half for the next meeting. Undertake no more than the class can do thoroughly.

2. If possible, use enlarged copies of the map and major charts appearing in this book at the appropriate class meetings.

3. Insist that as far as possible members of the class study the lesson at home and bring to the class written answers to the printed questions.

1 & 2 SAMUEL

A SELF-STUDY GUIDE

Irving L. Jensen

MOODY PRESS
CHICAGO

Scripture quotations, unless noted otherwise, are from the King James Version.

The use of selected references from various versions of the Bible in this publication does not necessarily imply publisher endorsement of the version in its entirety.

Cover photo: The Ruins of Ancient Shiloh

ISBN: 0-8024-4476-8

1 2 3 4 5 6 Printing/EP/Year 95 94 93 92 91

Printed in the United States of America

4. Briefly review the previous work at the beginning of each meeting.

5. Insist that the members of the class think and study for themselves. Give them opportunity to express their thoughts and tell the lessons they have learned. Refuse simply to lecture to the class.

6. Constantly emphasize the importance of carefully looking up all Scripture references given in each lesson. This should not be neglected.

Lesson 1
Background and Survey

The book called 1 Samuel follows Judges and its companion Ruth appropriately, for it continues the history of Israel from the point Judges leaves it.

In the study of the book of Judges we saw Israel's repeated departures from God and the complete failure of the nation to conform to the ways of God in either worship or government. The book ends in utter confusion religiously and politically, with every man doing "that which was right in his own eyes" and with no sense of authority in the land. The last verse states, "In those days there was no king in Israel." That is, no man was the head of the nation, no voice commanded the obedience of the people, no prince served as commander-in-chief of all the tribes at one time in a nationwide program to subdue the enemies, and no one monarch unified the people under the banner of their sovereign Lord God.

It was always God's purpose to reign as King in the lives of the Israelites. A government so ordered is called a *theocracy* (from the Greek *theos*, "God"). Furthermore, in terms of organization, God desired to preserve the unity of His chosen people through the leadership of *one* ruler over all. That is what is called *monarchy* (from the Greek *monos*, "one"). God's design, therefore, called for the combination theocracy-monarchy (theocratic monarchy, or monarchic theocracy).

The years of the judges were years of spiritual decline for Israel, because the nation was increasingly putting God out of their lives. Thus they were untheocratic. When the time came (1 Sam. 8) that they felt their need for a king (monarchy), they had rejected the idea of God on the throne (theocracy). God objected to their request for a king not because He was against kings (monarchy) but because of their rejection of Him (theocracy): "They have rejected me, that I should not reign over them" (1 Sam. 8:7).

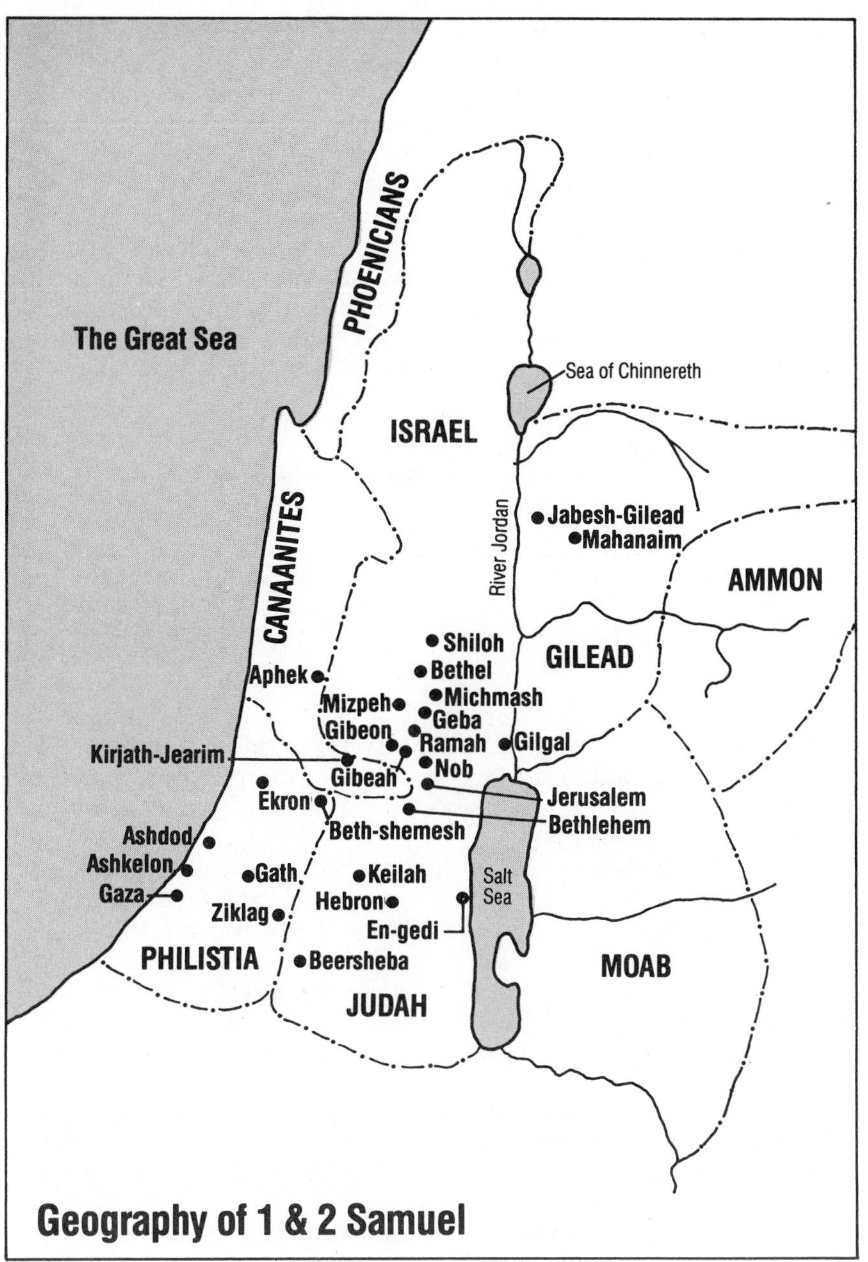
The Great Sea
PHOENICIANS
Sea of Chinnereth
ISRAEL
CANAANITES
River Jordan
Jabesh-Gilead
Mahanaim
AMMON
Shiloh
Bethel
GILEAD
Aphek
Michmash
Mizpeh
Geba
Gibeon
Ramah
Gilgal
Kirjath-Jearim
Nob
Gibeah
Ekron
Jerusalem
Bethlehem
Ashdod
Beth-shemesh
Ashkelon
Gath
Keilah
Salt
Sea
Gaza
Hebron
Ziklag
En-gedi
PHILISTIA
Beersheba
MOAB
JUDAH
Geography of 1 & 2 Samuel

God granted Israel kings but not without warning of consequences for dethroning Him as their King. Then, in His mysterious workings of grace and might, as God of history He used the people's kings as His channels of revelation, service, blessing, and justice. One of those whom He anointed as king was David, a "man after His own heart," who would be the grand type and forerunner of the messianic King. The two books of 1 and 2 Samuel describe the establishing of this Davidic kingdom in Israel.

It will be of help to you as you begin your study of 1 Samuel to see its place among the Old Testament books that describe Israel's history. Broadly speaking, the history of Israel as given in the Old Testament falls into four periods that may be remembered by four words, each beginning with the letter C, Camp, Commonwealth, Crown, Captivity. See the accompanying chart.

ISRAEL'S HISTORY BY PERIODS

CAMP	COMMONWEALTH	CROWN	CAPTIVITY
660 YEARS	360 YEARS	460 YEARS	160 YEARS
PENTATEUCH	JOSHUA JUDGES RUTH	SAMUEL KINGS CHRONICLES	EZRA NEHEMIAH ESTHER

1. The *Camp* period extended from the call of Abraham, the founder of the nation, to Moses' bringing the people up to the "gate" of Canaan, a period of about 660 years, the history of which is given in the Pentateuch.

2. The *Commonwealth* period extended from their entrance into Canaan under Joshua to the crowning of their first king, Saul, a period of about 360 years, the history of which is given in Joshua, Judges, and Ruth.

3. The *Crown* period extended from the crowning of their first king, Saul, to the Babylonian captivity, a period of about 460 years, the history of which is given in the six books of Samuel, Kings, and Chronicles.

4. The *Captivity* period, including the restoration, extended from the Babylonian captivity to the end of Old Testament history, a period of about 160 years, the history of which is told in Ezra, Nehemiah, and Esther.

You will find interesting descriptions of these periods of Israel's history in Psalms 78 and 79, as follows: under Moses, Psalm

78:5-54; under Joshua, Psalm 78:55; under the judges, Psalm 78:56-64; under the kings, Psalm 78:65-72; in captivity, Psalm 79:1-13.

I. BACKGROUND

Our procedure in studying a book of the Bible follows this order:

(a) Study of the book's background (authorship, setting, etc.)

(b) Study of the book's content—first making a survey of the whole and then analyzing the various parts.

In this lesson, background and survey will be the subjects for study. (This lesson may be studied in two different parts if so desired.)

A. Title

Samuel is one of the main characters in the story of 1 and 2 Samuel and may have been one of the authors of the books. Why was his name rather than the name of one of the other main characters chosen for the title? This may partly be explained by the fact that Samuel was the key character of 1 Samuel, and it was he who anointed the two other main characters, Saul and David, to be king. Add to this the high esteem in which he was held by the Jews who attached titles to the Bible books (the titles were not part of the original autographs). "Among the Jews he was regarded as a national leader, second only to Moses. As Moses delivered Israel from Egypt, gave them the law, and brought them to the very borders of the promised land, so Samuel was sent of God to deliver Israel when the nation's fortunes seemed almost hopeless. Spiritually and politically, the nation appeared virtually lost at the end of Eli's judgeship (cf. 1 Sam. 4:12-22; Ps. 78:59-64; Jer. 26:6). Under Samuel came a wonderful spiritual renovation and a new hope (1 Sam. 7)."[1]

B. Place in the Canon

In our English Bible 1 and 2 Samuel appear among the historical books. The earliest Hebrew Bibles considered the two books as one, among the Former Prophets (Joshua, Judges, Samuel, Kings). Notice the change of titles made over the years:

Hebrew Bible (B.C.): Samuel; Kings

Septuagint (B.C.): 1, 2 Kings; 3, 4 Kings

1. Frances Davidson, ed., *The New Bible Commentary* (Grand Rapids: Eerdmans, 1953), pp. 262-63.

Vulgate (A.D.): 1, 2 Kings; 3, 4 Kings
English Bible (A.D.): 1, 2 Samuel; 1, 2 Kings

Because 2 Samuel is intimately related to 1 Samuel, a brief outline combining both books follows. Note especially that the last half of 1 Samuel and the first chapter of 2 Samuel are part of one section in the outline for the simple reason that the story of Saul does not end until chapter 1 of 2 Samuel.

FIRST AND SECOND SAMUEL

ELI, the ARK, and SAMUEL	SAMUEL and SAUL	SAUL and DAVID	DAVID, KING over JUDAH	DAVID, KING over ALL ISRAEL
1 SAM. 1	9	16	2 SAM. 2	5 24

C. Author and Date

It is difficult to identify the author, or authors. Samuel could only have narrated the events that preceded his death (recorded in 1 Sam. 25). (That Samuel was a writer of at least one work is indicated by 1 Sam. 10:25.) Various suggestions of authorship or coauthorship include Abiathar, an attendant of David; Nathan and Gad (cf. 1 Chron. 29:29); and pupils from Samuel's school of the prophets. The detailed and vivid account of the happenings, with which these books abound, indicates that most of the narrative was written by men living at the time these things occurred rather than that the authors lived at a much later date.

The fact of joint authorship does not take away from the unity of the book as to its theme. Concerning all the writings of Scripture, one must continually recognize the supernatural moving of the Holy Spirit in the human writers, whoever and however many they were, to compose the holy writings.

Granting the possibility of Samuel's being one of the authors, the two books 1 and 2 Samuel were written some time between 1025 and 900 B.C.

D. Purposes

Three main purposes of 1 Samuel may be cited:

1. *Historical*

(a) To furnish a record of the transition from the era of judges to that of the monarchy (read Acts 13:20-21, noticing these three words: judges, prophet, king)

(b) To describe the influences of Samuel upon the life of Israel and upon many of their leaders

(c) To furnish a setting for the reign of David as described in 2 Samuel

2. *Typical or Symbolical*

The books of Samuel are rich in typical, or symbolical, truths. In many ways this Old Testament book foreshadows Christ in His offices of prophet, priest, and king.

In this history of the kings of Israel we see how utterly incapable man is of governing himself. The Bible and human history convince us that what the world needs is the universal reign of an Absolute Ruler who shall have infinite love, wisdom, and power. Such a Monarch is coming and, we believe, coming soon. But we are told in Scripture that before the true King comes there must come the Antichrist who, in the power of Satan, shall rule for a time. The establishing of the kingdom in Israel prefigures all this. David is a type of Christ; but before David comes Saul.

3. *Spiritual*

First Samuel shares this spiritual purpose with all Scripture. You will learn many spiritual lessons from this book. Among them is what is taught about prayer. Take time out now to look up these references: 1:10-28; 7:5-10; 8:5-6; 9:15; 12; 19-23; 28:6.

E. The Man Samuel

The name Samuel is from a Hebrew word that has been variously translated as: "the name of God," "his name is God," "his name is mighty," or "heard of God."

One is not surprised that the Jews have esteemed Samuel second to Moses among their leaders. The psalmist (Ps. 99:6), and God speaking to Jeremiah (Jer. 15:1), classified Samuel with Moses as an interceding priest. Samuel held the honor of being the last of the judges (1 Sam. 7:6, 15-17) and the first of the new order of prophets (1 Sam. 3:20; Acts 3:24; 13:20). The stature of the prophetic office during the years of the kingdoms can be traced back to the life and ministry of Samuel. He probably was the founder of the school of prophets (cf. 10:5).

Samuel was a giant among the men of God in biblical times. He lived to serve God, not to save himself. He knew without reservation that following the Lord with all the heart was the highest calling of any man or woman, boy or girl. He was holy and humble and kind. He sought not his own good but always the good of others. And when the day came for him to turn the reins of leadership over to another, he did it with grace and paternal commendation.

F. Some Distinctive Points of 1 Samuel

First Samuel contains many unique items. Some of them are:

1. It is the source of the oft-quoted words "Ichabod" ("the glory is departed" or "where is the glory?"), 4:21; "Ebenezer" ("hitherto hath the Lord helped us"), 7:12; and "God save the king" (10:24).

2. The word of the Lord is referred to as "precious" (3:1). Recall other things cited by the Bible as precious, such as: redemption (Ps. 49:8), death of the saints (Pss. 72:14; 116:15), God's thoughts (Ps. 139:17), and lips of knowledge (Prov. 20:15).

3. Reference is made to the school of the prophets, probably founded by Samuel (10:5; 19:18-24).

4. It is the first Old Testament book to use the phrase "Lord of hosts" (appears eleven times in the two books of Samuel: e.g., 1 Sam. 1:3).

5. Like the book of Judges, explicit reference to the law of Moses is lacking. But many of the items and activities inherent in the law (offerings, Tabernacle, Ark, Aaron, Levites, etc.) appear frequently.

6. An important place is given to the Holy Spirit and (as noted earlier) prayer.

7. In the early chapters much light is shed on Shiloh as the focal place of the national religion.

II. SURVEY

Now that you have seen something of the background of this book and have noted some of its highlights, you are ready for a "skyscraper" view of its composition as a whole. Such an acquaintance will help you learn the overall structure of the book for a point of reference in your later analytical studies of the various smaller parts. By way of illustration: a tourist visiting New York City for the first time would do well to view the city first from the top of the Empire State Building before going down and moving about the labyrinth of streets, subways, buildings, and parks.

Survey study is basically composed of two activities: reading and recording. Use the following guides:

1. Before you begin to read, notice the accompanying chart with blank spaces for each chapter of the book. Make a note in your Bible that extra segments begin at 2:11 and 21:10; and that 4:1*b*, 7:3, and 28:3 replace 4:1, 7:1, and 28:1 as starting points.
2. With pencil or pen in hand, begin reading the book. You need not read every word of each chapter, but you should read enough so that you know the general content of each chapter. After read-

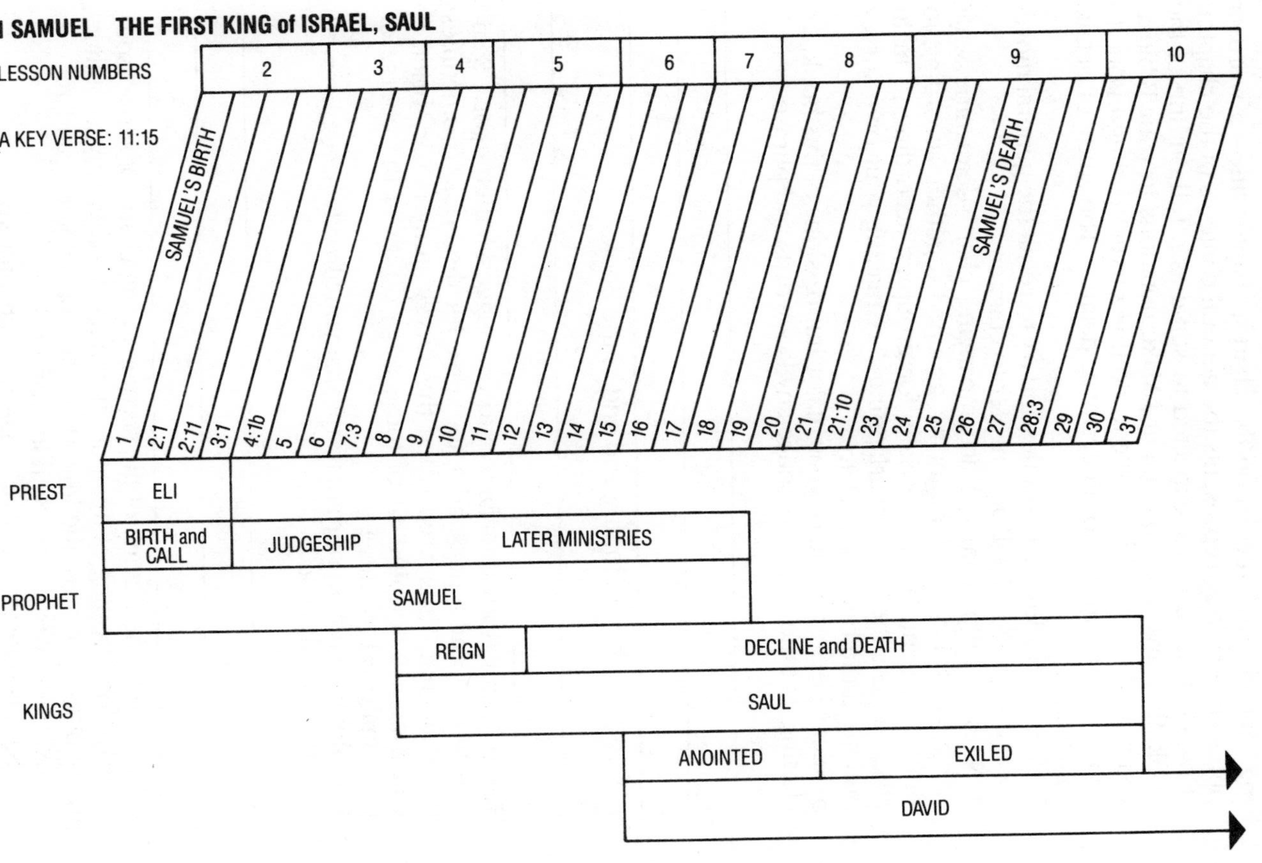
1 SAMUEL THE FIRST KING of ISRAEL, SAUL
LESSON NUMBERS
2
3
4
5
6
7
8
9
10
A KEY VERSE: 11:15
SAMUEL'S BIRTH
SAMUEL'S DEATH
1
2:1
2:11
3:1
4:1b
5
6
7:3
8
9
10
11
12
13
14
15
16
17
18
19
20
21
21:10
23
24
25
26
27
28:3
29
30
31
PRIEST
ELI
BIRTH and CALL
JUDGESHIP
LATER MINISTRIES
PROPHET
SAMUEL
REIGN
DECLINE and DEATH
KINGS
SAUL
ANOINTED
EXILED
DAVID

ing each chapter, record on the chart a chapter title—a word or phrase that at least represents the general contents of the chapter. (Chapter titles are not expected to serve as a full outline of the book; they are clues to content.) Make notations in your Bible as you read. You should be able to do this survey reading in one to two hours if you do not linger over details. (The study of details comes later.)

3. Next, read your chapter titles and try to recall the general movement of the narrative from chapter to chapter.

4. Without help from the accompanying chart, determine what chapters of 1 Samuel might be grouped together according to similar content. Look especially for grouping according to main characters. Is there any overlapping? Try making your own survey outline of the book on a chart.

5. Record below some of your major impressions of this book, including its tone. Did you notice any key words and phrases?

____

____

____

6. Compare the beginning and end of the book.

____

____

7. From your study thus far, could you suggest a theme for 1 Samuel? What about a title and a key verse for the book? (Sometimes these are not discovered when the survey study is very brief. If you cannot determine all of these now, do so in the course of your analytical studies.)

8. Write out a few important truths that you already have observed in your study thus far.

____

____

____

9. Now study the outline of the accompanying chart. Observe especially the overlapping of the four characters. Another way to outline the book is to observe the important place of chapters 9 and 16:

Samuel gives way to Saul in chapter 9.

Saul is rejected in favor of David in chapter 16.

With this in mind, the outline might be made to look something like this:

1	9	16 — 31
SAMUEL —prophet, priest, judge	SAUL —man after man's heart	DAVID —man after God's heart
—birth —childhood —judgeship	—choice —reign —rejection	—anointing —pursuit —exile

The shortcoming of such an outline is that no recognition is made of the obvious overlappings of the biographies. Let us now diagram this overlapping in a different way, showing the contrasting lives (upward and downward) of the main characters:

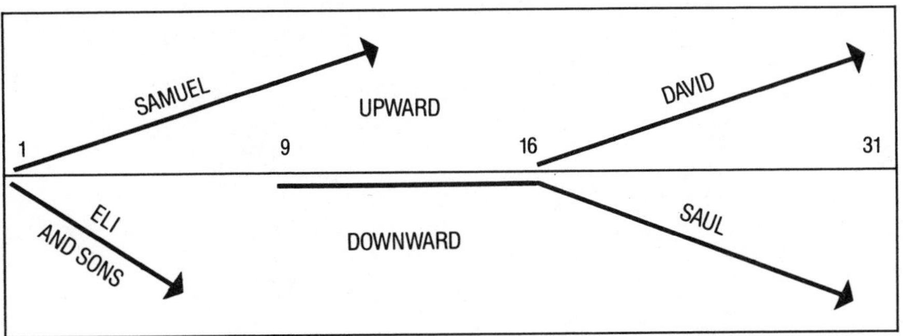

Various titles might be given this book. You may have already arrived at your own title (as discussed above). The one we are using in this study guide is: THE FIRST KING OF ISRAEL, SAUL. (The title we shall assign to 2 Samuel is a companion title: THE SECOND KING OF ISRAEL, DAVID.) The justifications for such a title are: Though Samuel is the key character of the book and though David excels Saul in heart and deeds in the last half of the book, the main point of the narrative is that it was at this time that the people first sought and crowned a king over them. That king was Saul; though not many good things could be written about him, he was Israel's first king and serves as the focal point of the book.

The time covered by 1 Samuel is perhaps one hundred years or more. It begins with the birth of Samuel (chap. 1) and ends with the death of Saul (chap. 31). Samuel was called "old" at the time Israel demanded a king (8:5; 12:2), and Saul reigned forty years after he was crowned.

III. SUMMARY

The book of 1 Samuel, of anonymous authorship, is the fourth historical volume of the Old Testament. It serves as a transition book, narrating the biographies of the last judge, Samuel, and the first king, Saul. But it takes the reader one step further in Israel's history by relating the early years of the life of David, who then is the main character of 2 Samuel.

Lesson 2 *1 Samuel 1:1–4:1a*

Samuel's Birth and Call

The first three chapters of 1 Samuel relate much about the transitional years between the judges and the kings. Two facts are prominent: corruption had defiled the *priesthood*, and there was a vital need for the voice and authority of the *prophet*. In your study of this section you will find many warm and challenging truths that are of timeless and universal application.

I. ANALYSIS

Read the Bible text carefully and prayerfully. As you read, underline words and phrases that you will want to examine more closely after the reading. Notice that 4:1*a* as the concluding sentence of this section serves as a fitting climax to all that precedes it.

One of the most obvious aspects of the author's composition of these chapters is the overlapping of two stories. Of course the overlapping is due to the interrelationships of the stories. The two stories involve:

(a) Samuel and his parents
(b) Eli and his sons

Your analysis should include how the narratives are woven together. As you prepare to read the passage again, mark in your Bible paragraph divisions given on the accompanying chart.

As you read each paragraph, record on the chart with as few words as possible the part played by Samuel or his parents and the part played by Eli or his sons. Then proceed with the following suggestions for study:

1. Study the outline, *Rise of a Prophet.*

2. Record on the chart your own outline concerning the fall of a dynasty of priests. Why are the sons of Eli introduced in the first paragraph?

____

1 SAMUEL 1:1—4:1a

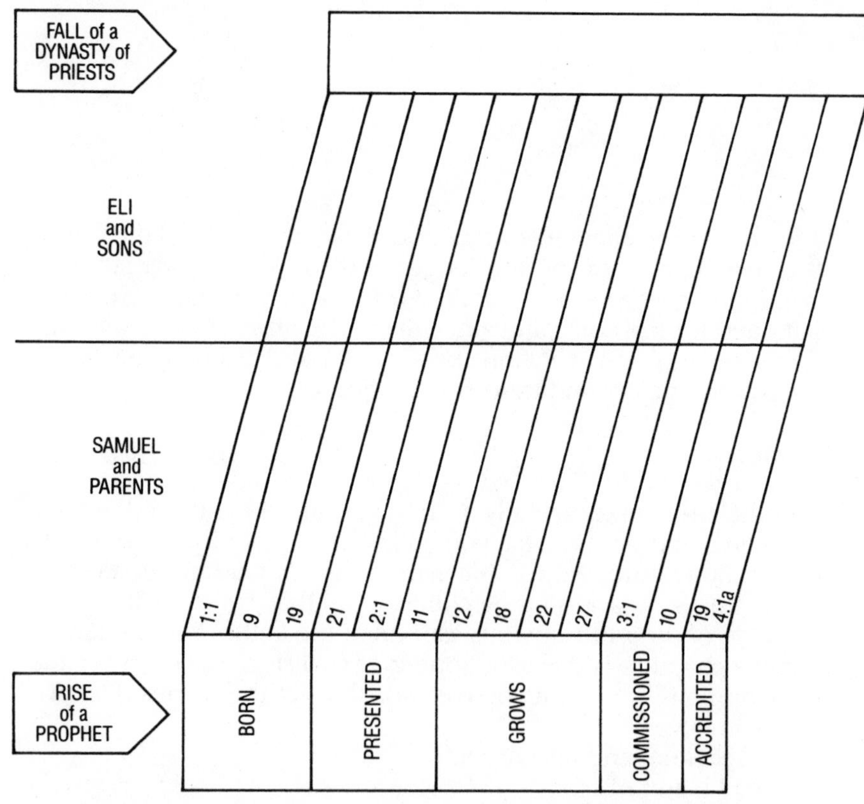

3. How does paragraph 2:11 serve as a transitional paragraph?

____

____

____

4. How does the last paragraph serve as a climax to the story?

____

____

5. List some of the contrasts you observe in this narrative.

6. Did Eli serve Hannah and Elkanah well as a priest?

7. See 1:1-8. Locate on the map (p. 7) Ramah (Ramathaim) and Shiloh. If possible, consult a Bible dictionary for a description and history of Shiloh. Notice how this first paragraph introduces the elements of the narrative's plot: parents of Samuel, priests whose dynasty would end, plight of Hannah.

8. see 1:9-18. What is shown here of grief and a broken spirit?

How does this account for the vow made?

9. See 1:19-28. Recalling the possible meanings of the name *Samuel* (Lesson 1), account for the name in the context.

Compare "I have asked him of the Lord" (1:20) with "I have lent him to the Lord" (1:28). (Instead of "lent," *American Standard Version* reads "granted"; Berkeley Version reads "turned him back.")

10. See 2:1-10. Analyze Hannah's prayer. What is the major tone of the prayer?

List the various attributes that Hannah ascribes to God.

Were her words expressed at random, or do you observe some order here?

Notice the tenses of the verbs. Where does the future tense appear?

What lessons can be learned from this prayer?

11. See 2:12-36. What was Eli's sin? (Cf. 2:29 with 3:13.)

What strong warning does this furnish to Christian leaders and parents today?

Study carefully the words following "Thus saith the Lord" (2:26-36). What may be learned about God from this?

12. See 3:1-18. This is the story of Samuel's first commission to speak a message for God. About how old was Samuel at this time? (See 3:1.)

What is meant by 3:7?

What was the message that God wanted Samuel to deliver?

What was Samuel's first reaction?

How was this a true test for the office of prophet?

What basically was the ministry of an Old Testament prophet?

___

___

___

13. See 3:19–4:1*a*. List the traits of a good prophet, as shown in these few verses.

___

___

___

Relate 3:21 to "the word of the Lord was precious [rare] in those days" (3:1).

___

___

(Note: The phrase "open vision" may be read as "broken open vision"—that is, "one broken open like an alabaster bottle of perfume and the fragrance dispersed."[1]

The key phrase of 3:21 is "in Shiloh." This was the location of the Tabernacle where the priests ministered. From your study of these chapters, what had happened to the ministry of the priesthood?

___

___

What then is significant about 3:21?

___

___

14. Before reading the COMMENTS section, write out a list of the prominent spiritual lessons taught by these chapters.

___

___

___

___

___

1. Merrill F. Unger, *Unger's Bible Handbook* (Chicago: Moody, 1966), p. 187.

II. COMMENTS

A. The Birth of Samuel

When one sees a man who has done a great work, it is natural to inquire about the kind of a home from which he came and especially about his mother. Often the influence of a mother is behind all his greatness. This was true in Samuel's case. His mother, Hannah, was a noble woman and a model mother. Samuel was fortunate to have such a mother to teach and pray for him.

Note carefully, in Hannah's prayer (1:10-11), just what she asked and what she promised. She pleaded for a man child, whom she promised to give back to the Lord as a Nazirite. (See Num. 6:1-5.) It may be that Hannah looked beyond her longings for a child and saw how desperately the nation needed a man in this time of religious decline who would be separated wholly unto God, as the Nazirite vow provided. If so, her prayer was remarkably selfless. She was praying for the good of the nation and the glory of God's name. God can always trust His children with gifts that they are willing to give back to Him. Hannah's prayer was heard, and the next year Samuel was born. True to her word, she gave the boy to the Lord. As soon as he was about three years of age and old enough to be separated from her, she brought him to Shiloh and left him with the priest. One can imagine her mixed emotions as she made the journey home, missing sorely the sweet laughter and baby prattle of her only son.

Hannah had given her dearest treasure to the Lord. But our generous Lord always favors true devotion to Himself. As her reward, the Lord gave Hannah other sons and daughters. In addition, think of the joy and satisfaction that Hannah had in later years when her beloved little son had grown to manhood and all the nation acknowledged his leadership and gave him honor.

It always pays to return to the Lord what He first has given us, whether it is time, money, service, talent, or children.

B. Hannah and Eli

The early chapters of 1 Samuel present some striking contrasts between the two parents, Hannah and Eli. One was a humble, obscure woman; the other a prominent man in the priestly office. One had the joy of seeing her child grow up noble, useful, honored, and blessed of God; the other had the pain of seeing his children disgrace the name they bore and the office they occupied. Hannah talked with God, giving Him praise and thanksgiving; Eli talked with his vile sons in a feeble reproof for their wickedness. Hannah was blessed by the Lord and given more children; Eli was rebuked by the Lord and had the sentence of death pronounced upon his children.

Why did all this happen? Was not Eli, as well as Hannah, a true worshiper of God? Yes, but notice the difference in their attitude toward God. Hannah's attitude was that of honoring God and giving Him, His work, and His glory first place. Eli honored his sons above God in the matter of offerings (2:29). In His dealings with these two parents God was following out the principle that He states in 1:30: "Them that honour me I will honour, and they that despise me shall be lightly esteemed."

C. Samuel's Call

Samuel is one of many who have been called in early youth to serve God. He may have been no older than twelve when God called him by name one night and gave him a message for Eli.

A prophet's task is always a hard one. If he is faithful he must deliver not only the joyous but often the most unwelcome messages from the Lord. The life of the prophet Jeremiah abounds in illustrations of this. It was no easy message that Samuel was given as his first to deliver: to tell the fond old father the woeful words of 3:11-14. At first Samuel hesitated, out of fear. But with the persuadings of Eli, he gave the message.

By the faithful discharge of this first work given him, Samuel proved his fitness for the prophetic office. As he grew up, all Israel recognized him as a prophet of the Lord; and through him the Lord again spoke to His people.

III. SUMMARY

1. Samuel was born
2. "And Samuel grew" (3:19).
3. "And the word of Samuel came to all Israel" (4:1).
4. "And the Lord was with him" (3:19).

Lesson 3

1 Samuel 4:1b–7:2

The Ark of the Lord

When four thousand soldiers of Israel were slain on the battlefield by the Philistines, the big question was: Why has God done this to us? (4:3). The elders of Israel recalled victories of earlier generations, like the siege of Jericho (Joshua 6:6ff.), when the Ark of the Lord—a chest containing the tables of the law—was given a prominent place in the midst of the Israelite hosts. Hence the elders' advice to bring the Ark into battle (1 Sam. 4:3).

Such is the setting of the story of this lesson. Some questions may immediately come to your mind, such as:

1. Was the prophet Samuel, so recently accredited as a voice for the Lord, sought for counsel at this time? The text does not say, but we may surmise he was not consulted. The name *Samuel* does not appear once in this long passage. This is all the more significant when we observe that the sentence just preceding this entire passage records an effective ministry of Samuel: "And the word of Samuel came to all Israel" (4:1*a*).

2. Were the priests of no avail? The passage furnishes the answer and the reasons, confirming what we already have learned in the previous lesson.

3. What does an ark have to do with the fate of people? This is a key question for your study of this passage. There are many interesting answers.

Before proceeding with your analysis, it would be profitable to observe the setting of this passage in the structure of the first eight chapters of 1 Samuel. This is shown by the chart on the next page. Some things to notice about this chart are:

1. There is no mention of Samuel in the text of the middle section. Hence the designation SILENT YEARS.

2. The duration of the first section, CHILDHOOD YEARS, is based on the word "child" of 3:1.

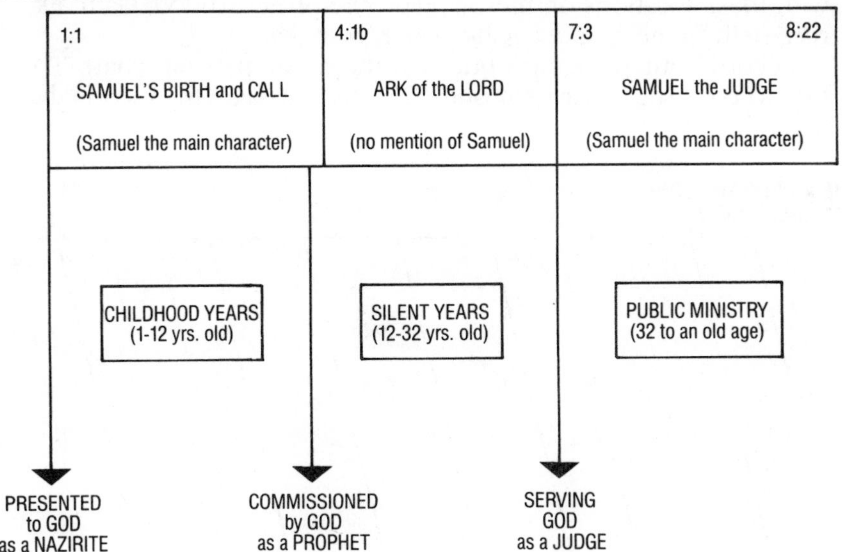

3. The twenty-year duration of the second section, SILENT YEARS, is based on 7:2 (see later in this lesson). Actually the Ark was in the hands of the Philistines for only seven months (6:1).

4. The text first shows Samuel ministering as a judge of Israel in section 7:3–8:22. (Of course he continued to serve after 8:22, but then the head of the nation—beginning at chap. 9—is a king.)

5. Observe how similar this three-phased life is to that of Jesus and also of John the Baptist.

I. ANALYSIS

Mark paragraph divisions in your Bible according to the accompanying chart. Read the passage in one sitting. Follow the procedures of reading and recording as suggested in Lesson 2. Let these become a regular part of your study habits.

1. Underline in your Bible every reference to the Ark. Count the references if you wish. Obviously the *ark of the Lord* is the main subject of these chapters. Notice the various ways the Ark is described, e.g., "ark of God," "ark of the covenant of the Lord." As a refresher, consult a Bible dictionary for a description and history of the Ark. Study the following references that indicate what the Ark symbolized for the Israelites: Exodus 30:6; Numbers 10:33-36; Joshua 3.

2. Since geography is involved in the action, acquaint yourself with these locations on the map (p. 7): Aphek, Ashdod, Gath, Ekron, Bethshemesh, Gaza, Ashkelon, Kirjath-jearim.

3. Record your paragraph titles on the accompanying chart. Try first to construct your own outline of the passage; then study the ones shown.

THE ARK OF THE LORD
1 SAMUEL 4:1b—7:2

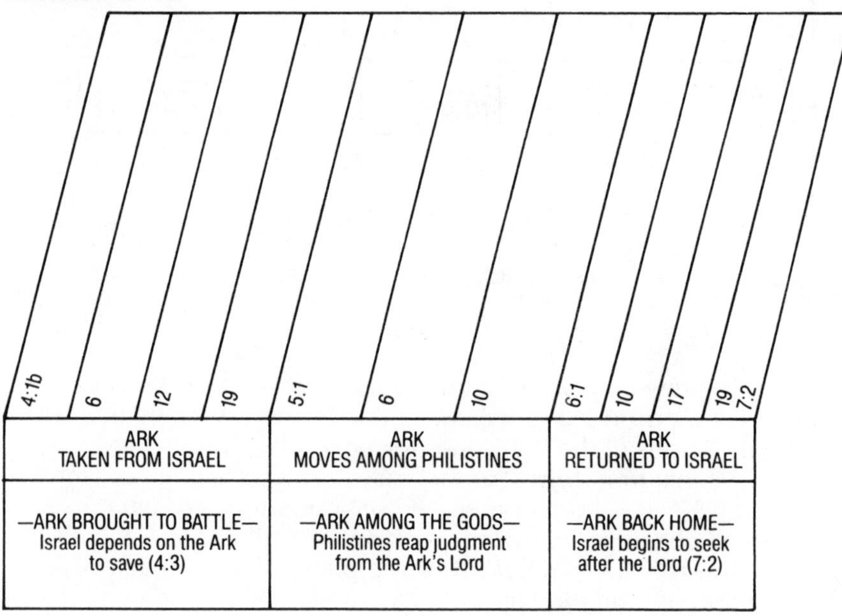

4:1b
6
12
19
5:1
6
10
6:1
10
17
19
7:2
ARK
TAKEN FROM ISRAEL
ARK
MOVES AMONG PHILISTINES
ARK
RETURNED TO ISRAEL
—ARK BROUGHT TO BATTLE—
Israel depends on the Ark
to save (4:3)
—ARK AMONG THE GODS—
Philistines reap judgment
from the Ark's Lord
—ARK BACK HOME—
Israel begins to seek
after the Lord (7:2)

4. Compare 4:3 and 7:2, as to where the Israelites were turning for help. For clarity, read 7:2 thus: "During a long period while the ark remained in Kirjath-jearim, for twenty years the whole house of Israel was seriously seeking the Lord" (Berkeley Version).

5. See 4:1*b*-11. Contrast the Israelites' confidence (4:5) with the Philistines' fear (4:7). What was the outcome of each.

____

____

____

"Let us fetch the ark . . . that . . . it may save us" (4:3). What was the sin here?

____

6. See 4:12-18. What were the four facts reported to Eli (4:17)?

____

____

____

____

What is the significance of the order in which they were spoken to him?

____

____

What was closest to Eli's heart as of this time?

____

Support your answer with evidence from the text.

7. See 4:19-22. What was the basis for Phinehas' wife's view of Israel's status? (vv. 21-22).

____

____

The Hebrew name *Ichabod* means literally: "Where is the glory?" *The Wycliffe Bible Commentary* suggests that here the word "glory" may have been used as a substitute for "God." Hence, "Where is God?"

Note: Some Bible scholars believe that the victory of the Philistines (4:10) was followed by the desolation of Shiloh. "Though the historical books are silent about this tragedy, it was still far from forgotten in Jeremiah's day (Jer. 7:12, 14; 26:6).[1] Consult an exhaustive Bible concordance to note the absence of the words "ark" and "Shiloh" from the text of 1 Samuel after this section, 4:1*b*–7:2.

8. See 5:1-5. Who is the all-powerful one identified here?

____

How is he directly identified in the next two paragraphs (5:6-9; 5:10-12)?

____

____

____

1. Charles F. Pfeiffer and Everett F. Harrison, eds., *The Wycliffe Bible Commentary* (Chicago: Moody, 1962), p. 279.

9. See 6:1-18. These verses present contrasting pictures of the Philistines and the Lord. Identify them.

____

____

10. See 6:19–7:2. How is 7:2 a climax to the entire story of this passage?

____

____

What had the Israelites finally concluded regarding the Ark and regarding the Lord?

____

____

11. Review the highlights of this story, and then write out a list of some spiritual applications that may be made on the basis of the text.

____

____

____

____

II. COMMENTS

A. The Ark Taken

The Ark of the Covenant was the principal part of the Tabernacle. Without the Ark, which was the symbol of God's presence, the Tabernacle was like a body without life, and its whole service was rendered useless.

The Ark was not lost by accident. One might say that it was literally thrown away. Under Samson the Philistines had only been temporarily subdued, and at the time of our lesson they were again aggressively hostile. The Israelites went forth to battle against them (4:1), but we hear nothing of their asking counsel of the Lord. We see no God-appointed leader. It was of natural consequence that "when they joined battle, Israel was smitten before the Philistines" (4:2).

This is what Moses had told his brethren they might expect if they would not obey the Lord (Deut. 28:15, 25). But these Israelites did not seem to understand the cause of defeat, and they asked: "Why has the Lord smitten us today before the Philistines?" (4:3). If they had been diligently reading the books that Moses wrote and left for them as they had been told to do, they would have understood why they were smitten. They consulted together and came up with this plan, "Let us fetch the ark of the covenant of the Lord out of Shiloh unto us, that, when it cometh among us, it may save us out of the hand of our enemies" (4:3). They put their confidence in the Ark itself, which was only the *symbol* of God's presence. They were trusting in the symbol rather than in the One symbolized.

B. The Ark Among the Philistines

Evidently God sought two ends in allowing the capture of the Ark: first, the discipline of Israel; and second, the vindication of His supremacy over the gods of the nations. Therefore, in these chapters we see Israel brought to repentance, and the gods of the heathen brought to ridicule. The possession of the Ark proved to be a curse rather than a blessing to the Philistines. This was because God, for whose presence the Ark stood, was not given His proper place.

God's presence among men will either bless or judge. God blesses when men receive Him and yield to Him; He judges when men reject Him and rebel against Him. The Philistines were convinced of the superior power of the God of the Hebrews, yet they did not yield and take Him for their God. They thought they could escape Him. They preferred Dagon, and so the continuing presence of the Ark in their midst could bring nothing but judgment.

C. The Ark Returned

For seven months the Ark remained with the Philistines, and they were months filled with suffering, disease, and death. "Send away the ark," was their cry. Note their familiarity with the circumstances of Israel's exodus from Egypt and how they sent the Ark away with gifts even as the Egyptians had given jewels of gold and silver to the departing Israelites (6:6-8). Note also the miraculous: the cows going against nature in leaving their young (6:12). God proved Himself to be the God of creation, supreme above all natural instincts. God obviously revealed Himself to other peoples as well as to the chosen nation of Israel.

The Ark was eventually moved to Kirjath-jearim and deposited in the house of Abinadab, where it remained for a long time (the total time of its stay at this place was more than twenty years, as shown by 2 Sam. 6:2-4 and 1 Chron. 13). During the first years of that period people were beginning to see their need of the Lord, and were "seriously seeking the Lord" (7:2, Berkeley Version). A footnote to 7:2 in the Berkeley Version reads, "Samuel seems to have begun his judgeship of Israel that twentieth year, probably at the age of thirty, like Jesus and John the Baptist."

The story of our next lesson begins here.

III. SUMMARY

In these chapters about the Ark of the Lord, God is shown in His dealings with the Israelites and the Philistines.

God allowed the Israelites to be defeated in battle because they were trusting in the Ark rather than in Him. He wanted to show them that their Savior was a Person to be loved, not a thing (ark) to be carried.

God sent the Philistines judgment despite their victories, because they revered their gods more than Him. He wanted to show them that their Creator was a Person to be feared, not a thing (statue) to be made.

Lesson 4

1 Samuel 7:3–8:22

Samuel the Judge

Israel's national and spiritual life were disrupted and confused by the temporary loss of the Ark, the decimation of their armies, the destruction of Shiloh, and the continuing oppressions of the Philistines. But they were beginning to see that the judgments upon them were for their sins, so they were "seriously seeking" the Lord (7:2). At this time Samuel, whose office they had once honored (3:20), sent a message to all the tribes, calling for a revival of heart and return to the Lord. To be more explicit, he called for a conference of the leaders of all Israel to be held at the city of Mizpeh. So begins the story of this section of 1 Samuel.

Before you analyze these two chapters, review the chapters of 1 Samuel already studied. Observe especially the changing spiritual climate of Israel during these years. The following diagram shows some of the major developments:

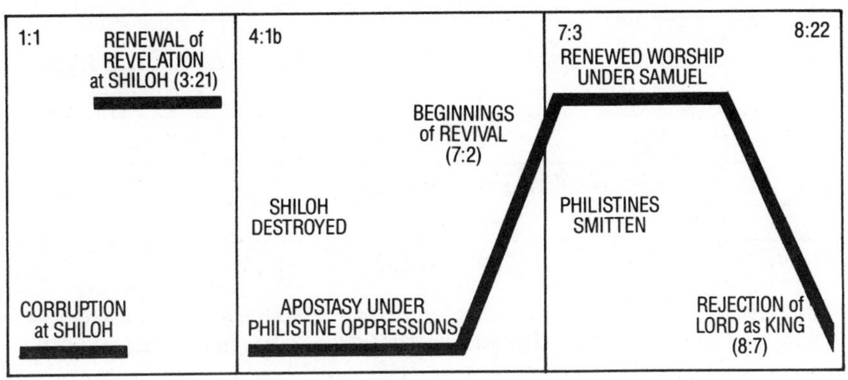

Review also the survey chart of 1 Samuel 1:1–8:22 given on page 25.

I. ANALYSIS

This passage should be scrutinized closely. It is a key passage in 1 Samuel for at least two reasons:

(a) It is the only passage recording the service of Samuel in his official capacity as judge *over* all Israel (he served as a judge *in* Israel "all the days of his life," even during Saul's reign as king);

(b) This is a turning point in Israel's history from a theocracy to a monarchy.

1. Mark these paragraph divisions in your Bible: 7:3, 7, 13; 8:1, 4, 10. Also look up the locations of these places on the map: Mizpeh, Gilgal, Bethel, and Beersheba.
2. After your preliminary reading and associated studies, record your observations on an analytical chart similar to the one shown. Record paragraph titles and key words and phrases. Observe the geography of each paragraph and complete the list begun on the accompanying chart (with Mizpeh).
3. Compare the beginning and end of this segment. For example, observe:

"And Samuel spake . . . *return* unto the Lord" (7:3).

"And Samuel said . . . *go* unto (your) city" (8:22).

4. Identify the *main subject of each paragraph.* Try to make different outlines for this segment. Notice any grouping of paragraphs as to content. Record all your studies on your analytical chart.
5. Make a character study of Samuel throughout the segment.
6. Study the outlines shown on the accompanying chart.
7. See 7:3-6. What were the four conditions stipulated for deliverance?

____

____

____

____

Did the Israelites fulfill the conditions?

____

8. See 7:7-12. What did the Israelites need to learn?

____

How appropriate was the name of verse 12? (Ebenezer means "stone of help.")

____

____

SAMUEL THE JUDGE
1 SAMUEL 7:3—8:22

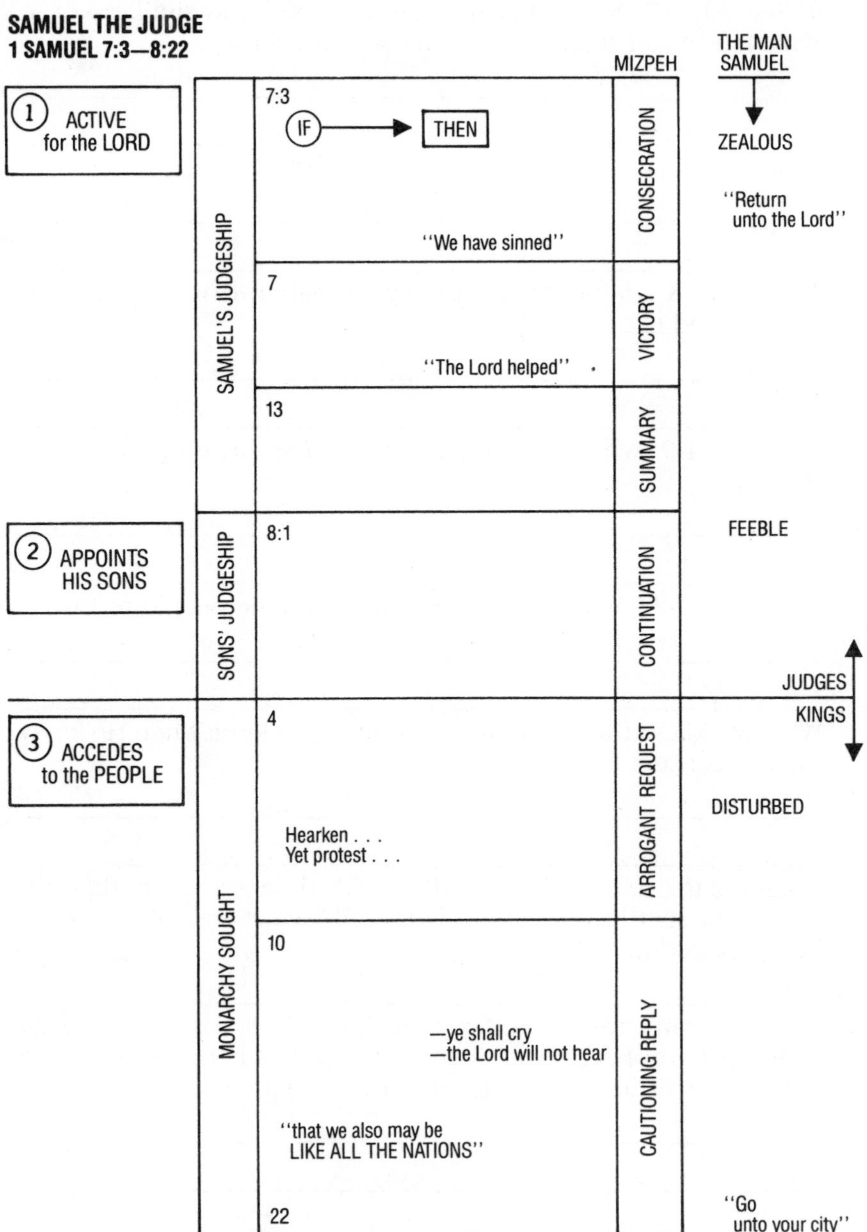

MIZPEH
THE MAN SAMUEL
1 ACTIVE for the LORD
SAMUEL'S JUDGESHIP
7:3
IF
THEN
"We have sinned"
CONSECRATION
ZEALOUS
"Return unto the Lord"
7
"The Lord helped"
VICTORY
13
SUMMARY
2 APPOINTS HIS SONS
SONS' JUDGESHIP
8:1
CONTINUATION
FEEBLE
JUDGES
KINGS
3 ACCEDES to the PEOPLE
MONARCHY SOUGHT
4
Hearken . . .
Yet protest . . .
ARROGANT REQUEST
DISTURBED
10
—ye shall cry
—the Lord will not hear
"that we also may be LIKE ALL THE NATIONS"
CAUTIONING REPLY
22
"Go unto your city"

9. See 7:13-17. Notice the repetition of "all" and similar words. What kind of an altar do you suppose Samuel built?

How does this paragraph serve as a summary paragraph?

10. See 8:1-3. Samuel's sons had a good father. How is it that "his sons walked not in his ways"?

11. See 8:4-9. What was the people's *real* sin in wanting a king? (Cf. 8:20).

12. See 8:10-22. What manner of king would the people receive?

Why would God accede to their request for a king, when He knew the evil consequences?

Compare the setting of Psalm 106:15, "And he gave them their request; but sent leanness into their soul." What trait of Samuel is best revealed in 8:10-22?

13. When you have finished your analysis of this passage, meditate over what you have seen. Then write a list of some of the more important spiritual lessons taught by this segment.

II. COMMENTS

A. Samuel the Judge

While the Ark rested at Kirjath-jearim, the Philistine power over Israel remained unbroken. None but God could break it; but His people, in spite of the experiences of the past, were slow to realize this fact. When they at last turned their faces toward the Lord and began to lament after Him, Samuel told them what additional steps they had to take before God could deliver them. Their crying out to Him would have no effect unless they would turn to Him with their whole heart, put away their idols, and serve Him only (7:3). They took this advice, gathered for prayer, fasting, and confession, and a mighty revival resulted.

The first book of Samuel shows this man of God in the threefold office of priest, prophet, and judge. Each year he traveled in circuit to Bethel, Gilgal, and Mizpeh in order to judge Israel, but his home was in Ramah, his birthplace. His erecting the altar at Ramah was in the interest of his priestly ministry. The priesthood had declined, and the central sanctuary at Shiloh had been broken up. His devotions and sacrifices at this altar were no doubt personal, but they were also offered in behalf of his people whom he dearly loved.

Time passed, and Samuel became an old man. Holy and fruitful as his life and work had been, he had committed a sad error in making his sons judges over Israel (8:1-2). He had no right to do this. Priestly or apostolic succession without God's appointment is forbidden. God alone can call to service and give gifts for the ministry. Moreover, three sons of Samuel were not fit men to be in any place of authority. Their dishonesty and avarice made the people disgusted and dissatisfied, thus opening the way for them to voice the desire that had long been on their hearts.

B. Israel's Demand for a King

The secret was out at last. Although the Israelites used the impiety of Samuel's sons as an excuse and although that may have been the immediate cause, the truth of the matter was that they wanted to be like the neighboring nations. They refused to be a peculiar people any longer. They could not bear the place of separation. They wanted to be exactly what God wanted them *not* to be, "like all the nations." He had chosen Israel out of all the nations of the earth to be His special representatives. He had taken them into covenant relationship with Himself, placed them on a pinnacle above all the nations, and there He wanted them to stay and lift other nations to their level, not sink back to the level from which they had been taken and be "like all nations."

That is just the danger that threatens Christians today. Many cannot bear the thought of being considered different from those among whom they mingle. So they adopt worldly methods and join in worldly practices and customs until it is difficult to distinguish them from the unsaved. God does not want His people to be like other people. He wants them to be like Christ. There should be such a marked difference in their words and manner of life as compared with the ways of the world that all will recognize them as God's peculiar people.

Samuel was disturbed over this request for a king, and he took the matter to the Lord in prayer. God answered: "They have not rejected thee, but they have rejected me, that I should not reign over them" (3:7). God was not deceived. Looking into their hearts, He saw that they did not want Him to be their King. They were glad enough to have Him as their Deliverer, saving them from death and bondage in Egypt and from all the hostile nations. But they did not want Him to be King, controlling their lives. Many would like to have Christ for their Savior, delivering them from the death penalty of sin, but they do not want to let Him be King of their lives and control their thoughts, words, and acts. But there is no salvation without true surrender.

God would grant Israel's request for human kings but not without first solemnly warning them of the consequences. They were not to make this decision ignorantly. So Samuel reasoned with them that God could look into the future as they could not and He knew what they could expect. Then he described the kind of king that would be theirs. Read verses 11-17, noting the frequency of the phrase "he will take." The impression of selfishness is predominant, being the leading characteristic of this king whom they wanted. And so it proved to be.

Even after God made the solemn declaration of verse 18, they willfully and stubbornly persisted: "Nay; but we will have a king over us; that we also may be like all the nations" (8:19-20).

So the die was cast; Israel entered another phase of her history.

III. SUMMARY

As a summary exercise, list about five highlights of this story, identifying the timeless universal principle involved in each.

Lesson 5

1 Samuel 9:1–12:25

Saul the King

Samuel was wiser than all the elders of Israel, and he knew that God would not bless a demand for the kind of king such as those who ruled the neighboring heathen nations. But Israel did not yield to Samuel's persuasions. Thus began the hardest years of his life—hard because of the tests they brought. But Samuel remained a spiritual prince throughout. As leader of the nation, he showed humility in bowing out with grace. As a servant of God, he utterly obeyed God's directions to appoint a king, knowing—with God—the hardships that would come. And as a brother of the Israelites, he continued to show genuine love for his own, faithfully interceding on their behalf (cf. 12:23).

Samuel did not move off the scene completely when Saul the king was brought on. But the era of judges had passed, and kingdom rule had begun. And at least there was a good beginning to the new era, as your study of these four chapters will reveal.

Before reading the chapters, study the accompanying outline of the remaining chapters of 1 Samuel for survey purposes. Recall from Lesson 1 that Saul had not been king for long when he began treading the downward path.

I. ANALYSIS

There are three main parts to this passage:

Chapter 9: Samuel's message to Saul
Chapter 10-11: CORONATION OF SAUL
Chapter 12: Samuel's charge to the people

The two middle chapters are the key chapters, since coronation is the key subject; but all four chapters record vital aspects of Israel's experiences at this time.

Read through the four chapters paragraph by paragraph, following the study procedures you have been using for the earlier

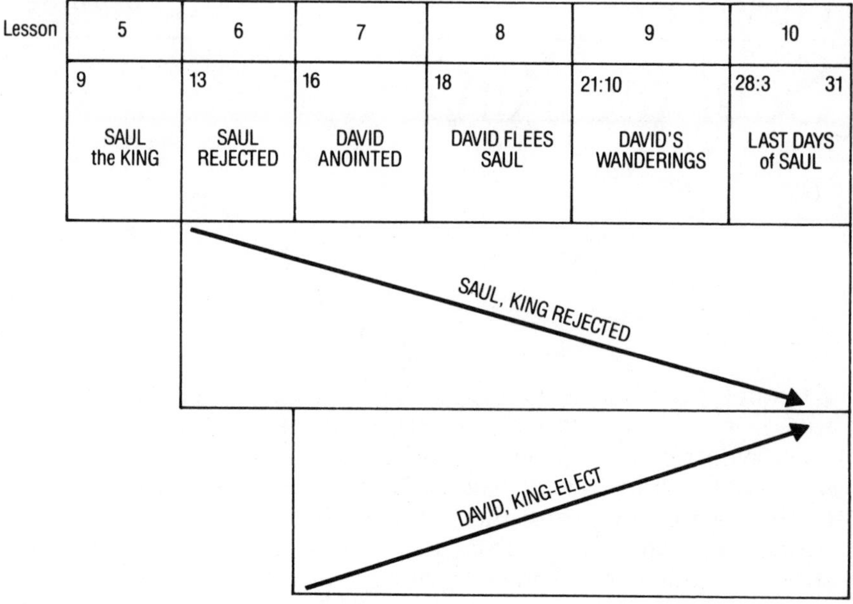

lessons. Be sure to underline in your Bible the many strong phrases of these chapters. They will suggest profitable applications in your later studies.

It will be helpful for you to see the organization of these chapters. The accompanying rectangles represent the three units shown above. Study the outlines already provided, but also work out an outline of your own. Use the blank spaces to record key words and phrases. Record paragraph titles in upper right-hand corner of each paragraph box (e.g., *Choice man, Seer*). Jot down whatever you see in the passage that strikes you or suggests some important thought.

Continue your analysis by searching the text for answers to the following questions:

1. Compare the credentials of Saul the young man (9:1-2) with those of Samuel the aged (12:1-5).

____

____

____

____

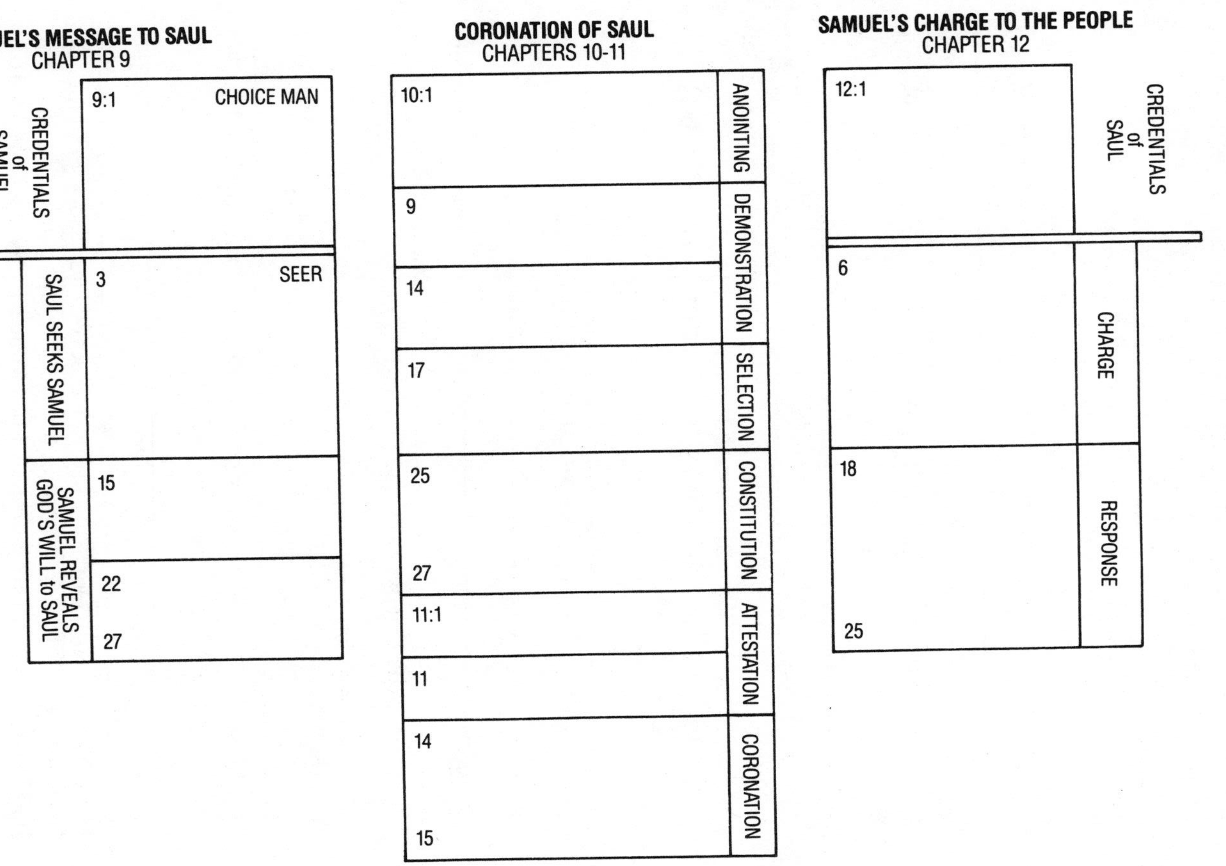

SAMUEL'S MESSAGE TO SAUL
CHAPTER 9
CREDENTIALS of SAMUEL
9:1
CHOICE MAN
SAUL SEEKS SAMUEL
3
SEER
SAMUEL REVEALS GOD'S WILL to SAUL
15
22
27
CORONATION OF SAUL
CHAPTERS 10-11
10:1
ANOINTING
9
14
DEMONSTRATION
17
SELECTION
25
27
CONSTITUTION
11:1
11
ATTESTATION
14
15
CORONATION
SAMUEL'S CHARGE TO THE PEOPLE
CHAPTER 12
12:1
CREDENTIALS of SAUL
6
CHARGE
18
25
RESPONSE

2. See 9:5-14. What aspect of the office of prophet does this paragraph reveal?

3. See 9:15-21. Study the subject of the sovereignty of God as taught here. For example compare 9:17 with 8:9.

Relate this sovereign will to Israel's desire (9:20) and Saul's reticence (9:21).

4. See 9:22-27. Try to imagine how much was revealed to Saul on the housetop (9:25) and later on the street (9:27).
5. See 10:1-8. How significant was the act of anointing? (10:1).

What are the three signs to which Samuel refers in 10:7?

What were the purposes of the signs (10:7)?

And the offerings (10:8)?

6. See 10:9-16. What is meant by "God gave him another heart"? (10:9). (Compare 10:6.)

How was Saul's prophesying (10:11) to serve later as a credential for his coronation? (As of this time, the people did not know that Saul had been informed by Samuel of the kingship—hence vv. 14-16.)

7. See 10:17-24. Observe the method of using lots to choose a king. Was chance or the Lord the determinant?

____

How did Samuel emphasize this?

____

8. See 10:25-27. We are not told what was written in this book (10:25), but it described "the manner of the kingdom" (not "the manner of the king" 8:9, 11). Since this was revered as an official document, it may have been the constitution of the new kingdom. (Read Deut. 17:14-20 for what light this passage sheds on this.)

9. See 11:1-13. In what sense did this victory vindicate the choice of Saul as king?

____

Account for Saul's words "after Saul and after Samuel" (11:7).

____

____

How did Saul interpret the victory? (11:13*b*).

____

10. See 11:14-15. Comment on each of these phrases:

"renew the kingdom"
"made Saul king"
"sacrifices of peace offerings"
"all . . . rejoiced greatly"

11. See 12:1-5. What was Samuel's purpose behind these words?

____

____

____

12. See 12:6-17. Study carefully the charge that Samuel delivered to the people. Note the various ways he exalted the Lord.

____

____

13. See 12:18-25. What was the people's response and Samuel's promise?

____

____

____

What does 12:22 teach about the Lord preserving a remnant?

---

14. From your study of these four chapters, what things at least gave a *promise* of a good reign for Saul?

---

15. Though Saul is the central character of this passage, Samuel has a leading role throughout. Cite examples of this.

Recall Hannah's words of 1:28.
16. List some important lessons about Christian leadership that may be learned from this section.

II. COMMENTS

A. Saul Appointed King

The first king of Israel was a choice young man in the prime of life. He was a physical giant, industrious, generous, honest, and modest. When Samuel presented him to the people for the first time, his appearance was prepossessing, partly because "he was higher than any of the people from his shoulders and upward" (10:23). He was, to be sure, an attractive prospect. Israel's sin was not that of choosing a base character to be their king. Their sin was basically that of wanting to be led in the ways of the nations around them, not in the ways of the Lord. If there was to be any hope for Israel, it was to be because they would obey the Lord in all their ways, and their king would do likewise.

The day came for Samuel to make public the mind of God concerning the new king. He gathered the nation at Mizpeh. There he reminded them of God's goodness and power and of their own mistake in preferring a human leader like those of the enemy nations. Then the lot was cast, and the choice fell upon

Saul. When Samuel introduced him, the people were delighted at his height and appearance. They went up a great shout, "God save the king" (literally, "Let the king live").

"Then Samuel told the people the manner of the kingdom" (10:25). This was probably based upon Moses' instructions regarding a king (Deut. 17:14-20). See how accurately Moses had predicted, before Israel ever entered Canaan, that there would come a time when they would demand a king. He had foretold just what they would give as their reason for wanting one (Deut. 17:14).

Saul, chosen by God, was now accepted by the people. But the occasion for taking his place at the head of the nation had not yet arisen, so he returned home and began to work in the field as usual. Presently the opportunity came.

B. Saul's Victory

The Ammonites encamped against Jabesh-gilead. Seeking peace, the men of the place asked the Ammonite king to make a covenant with them. But they received an insolent reply: "On this condition will I make a covenant with you, that I may thrust out all your right eyes, and lay it for a reproach upon all Israel" (11:2). The Ammonites would agree to a pact only on the condition of making the men of Jabesh-gilead impotent in warfare. (Cf. Judges 1:7-8.) Messengers reached Gibeah with news of the threat.

How the insult offered by the Ammonites aroused Saul's anger. These heathen Ammonites were proposing to put out the right eyes of God's people, thus making it a standing reproach to all Israel that they had not the power to resist. Could not Israel claim almighty power? The Spirit of the Lord came mightily upon Saul. Laying hold of his oxen, he cut them in pieces and sent the pieces throughout all Israel with the message "Whosoever cometh not forth after Saul and after Samuel, so shall it be done unto his oxen" (11:7).

The fear of the Lord came on all the people, and they rallied to Saul as one man, going against the Ammonites and utterly routing them. The people were wild with enthusiasm over the great victory. Assembling at Gilgal, they crowned Saul king (11:15). This was the real coronation day.

C. Samuel's Charge to the People

While the Israelites still were assembled at Gilgal, where they had enthusiastically crowned Saul as king, Samuel the man of God, now advanced in years, stood before them and addressed the representatives of the nation. Although all seemed to be going well thus far with their new king as leader, Samuel did not want them to forget that they had committed sin in demanding a king, and that God, in His mercy, was blessing them in spite of this mistake, not because of it. Responding to his address, the people were filled with fear and confessed that they had sinned in many ways other than in asking for a king. But they pleaded with Samuel to pray that the penalty of death would not fall upon them. Again Samuel assured them that all would be well if they would only continue following God.

III. SUMMARY

The highlights of these four chapters may be classified under three headings:

1. CREDENTIALS of Saul: good, but not necessarily revealing the *inner man*
2. SIGNS displayed: miraculous, revealing the almighty *hand of God*
3. INTERPRETATIONS AND APPEALS by Samuel: accurate and earnest, from a *true man of God*

See how many events of this narrative you can recall under each heading.

Lesson 6

1 Samuel 13:1–15:35

Saul Rejected

King Saul knew what God required of him as leader of His people, for Samuel had explained the options clearly to all Israel (12:13-25), Saul's tests came soon, and these chapters of First Samuel reveal that he failed.

The occasions for the tests were again those "thorns" in the side—the enemy hosts. The military outcome of the battles against the Philistines and the Amalekites was victory for Israel, but the more serious outcome was that Israel lost a king. Saul would continue to lead the people, but God had rejected him from being king (15:23).

I. ANALYSIS

First locate these places on the map: Gilgal, Geba, Michmash, and Bethaven. Wherever geography is involved in the Bible text, acquaint yourself with the locations.

Mark the paragraph divisions in your Bible as they appear below. Then read the passage, following your usual study patterns.

Construct a work sheet similar to the one shown here. As you read the Bible text paragraph by paragraph, record a short phrase (one to three words) that will indicate the main contents of the paragraph. After you have completed this, record observations under the other three columns, thus:

SAMUEL: show the part Samuel played as related to Saul
SAUL: identify the occasions of his sins
JONATHAN: show the part Jonathan played, and its bearing on Saul.

In your study, arrive at some outline of these three chapters. Here are some questions to lead you into further study of the text.

PARAGRAPH	MAIN POINT	SAMUEL	SAUL	JONATHAN
13:1				
5				
8				
15b				
19				
14:1				
6				
17				
24				
36				
47				
49				
52				
15:1				
4				
10				
17				
24				
32				
34				

1. See 13:1-4. Contrast this first paragraph with the last one (15:34-35).

Note that Jonathan ("Jehovah has given") is introduced here as the leader of 1,000 warriors. Jonathan was Saul's son (13:16). Who is the central figure of this paragraph?

2. See 13:5-7. Identify the sin of Israel here.

3. See 13:8-15. It is possible that Saul may have offered the burnt offering through the priest (Ahijah) or that the offering was legally made by some leader other than the priest (e.g., David, 2 Sam. 24:25; and Solomon, 1 Kings 3:4). If either was the case, what was the real sin of Saul? (Compare 10:8.)

(For a discussion of the problem of time reference arising out of 13:1, consult a commentary.) Analyze carefully the words of doom of 13:13-15.

4. See 14:1-46. Compare the characters of Jonathan and Saul.

What was Saul's sin in interrupting the priest (14:19)?

What was his sin in restraining his people from eating food (14:24)?

Observe Saul's rashness in 14:36-46. Compare Saul's decree (14:44) and the people's veto (14:45). What does this reveal of Saul's leadership?

5. See 14:47-52. This section stands apart from the rest of the narrative. What does it contribute to a full perspective of Saul's career?

___

___

___

6. Chapter 15. All the elements of Saul's career are to be found in this one event. Identify each of these in the story: commandment, disobedience, exposure, alibi, confession, judgment. In what sense does God repent (15:11)?

___

What are the many spiritual lessons taught in this chapter?

___

___

___

___

II. COMMENTS

A. Saul Fails in Crisis

Saul failed to trust in God, and for this he was rejected. Samuel's earlier instruction to him was that he should be at Gilgal at a prearranged time and wait there seven days until Samuel's arrival (10:8). Now the date on the calendar had arrived. This was a critical test for Saul. The Philistines were pitched for battle just a few miles to the west at Michmash. Some Israelites were fleeing out of fear; others who remained with Saul were trembling. Saul was trembling too; and when Samuel did not arrive on the seventh day, Saul proceeded to take things into his own hands. This was his downfall—taking his eyes off God (for the directions from Samuel represented the will of God) and trying to win by his own efforts.

The situation surely was critical and might seem to have called for prompt action, but in crises like this it is always better to wait on God than to act without, or against, His command. That was proved in this case. Saul had been distinctly instructed to wait for the man of God to arrive to conduct the ceremony of sacrifice in God's appointed way (10:8). But in offering the burnt offering himself, he presumed to tell God how He should do His work.

Saul was attempting to approach God, but he was ignoring God's appointed way of approach. In the same way many today seek access to God while ignoring His appointed way of access—faith in the shed blood of Jesus Christ.

In rejecting Saul, God was seeking "a man after his own heart" (13:14), whom He found in David. It is interesting at this point, in anticipation of reading about David later, to compare Saul and David in these respects. There is a marked contrast between the two men.

Whenever David committed sin and was charged with it, he humbly confessed his guilt, repented, and asked for forgiveness. But when Saul committed sin and was charged with it, he excused himself and stubbornly refused to give it up. Also, when God's will and God's plan about a thing were revealed to David, he would not interfere; but Saul paid no attention to God's revealed will and did everything in his power to promote his own plans. Because of this attitude, David was described as a man after God's own heart. Not that he was faultless but, as explained in Acts 13:22, he was willing to do God's will.

B. Saul and Jonathan

A sweet contrast to Saul's attitude toward God is offered us by his son Jonathan. Jonathan is one of the most beautiful characters in the Bible. Undaunted by the subject condition of his people (13:5-7), or the strength of the enemy (13:15*b*-23), he went out filled with faith in God, accompanied by his armor-bearer, who was also a man of faith, to attack the Philistines. God enabled them to slay twenty Philistines, and the enemy warriors and even the earth itself trembled because of their presence.

One might think that Saul would have seen the hand of God in all this and acknowledged His might. Instead, we see a more arrogant and impatient Saul. When the rumble in the camp of the reorganized Philistines grew louder and louder, he interrupted the priestly services (14:19), which he had earlier requested. In his eyes the arm of the flesh had priority. This was his reason for denying food to his fatigued warriors—"that I may be avenged on mine enemies" (14:24). Really, it was in spite of Saul's impatience that "the Lord saved Israel that day" (14:23).

C. Saul's Rejection Confirmed

In chapter 15 God gives Saul a final test. As one writer has commented, "It may be that an opportunity was thus given to retrieve his former error by an exact obedience."

Had he proved himself to be a new man at this opportunity, the rest of Saul's sad history might not have been written. Since Saul's initial disobedience, several years (possibly twenty) had elapsed, during which he had had successful military operations with the surrounding nations (14:47-48). Now (15:1-3) he was given a command to utterly destroy the Amalekites in fulfillment of God's words in Exodus 17:14.

Saul well understood the grounds on which the enemy was to be destroyed. But instead of implicitly obeying God's command, he and the people spared Agag and the best of the sheep, oxen, fatlings, and lambs and all that was good (15:9). This was willful, premeditated, and repeated disobedience on the part of Saul.

So, because Saul rejected the word of the Lord, the Lord rejected him from being king. Saul confessed his sin; but it was not genuine repentance of heart for he still offered an excuse (15:24), and he was still trying to preserve his own honor in the sight of the people (15:30).

Saul's usefulness was now at an end. From this point in the story David, whom God chose in his place, is kept prominently before us. Saul's continuing reign is traced in order to show how a man who will go his own way, instead of God's way, goes deeper and deeper into sin until the end is destruction.

III. SUMMARY

The following evaluation of Saul is adapted from a book by J. Barton Payne:[1]

GOOD POINTS	DEGENERATED INTO
striking appearance 9:2	pride 18:8
initiative 11:7	rebellion 20:31
bravery 13:3	recklessness 14:24
patriotic Spirit-filling 11:6	demon possession 16:14

1. *An Outline of Hebrew History* (Grand Rapids: Baker, 1954), p. 96.

Lesson 7 *1 Samuel 16:1–17:58*

David Anointed

Saul, the first king of Israel, was a man after *man's* heart; he proved to be a complete failure as a theocratic king. The second king of Israel, David, was a man after *God's* heart; he showed what God can do through a surrendered will.

David, the greatest of Israel's kings, is one of the most fascinating characters in the whole of Scripture. The study of his life is exceedingly instructive, whether we consider him as a man, a king, or a type of Christ.

Few men have had such varied experiences as David. First he was a shepherd on the hills of Judah; then a servant in King Saul's palace; later a successful warrior; finally a king. At different times he was poor and rich, hated and beloved, persecuted and honored, obscure and prominent, a sinner and a worshiper. But in every position and condition of life he knew what it was to trust in the Lord. And in these varied experiences David poured forth his heart to God in praises, thanksgivings, confessions, or petitions, many of which are preserved in the book of Psalms.

The choice of David as Israel's king was God's decision. Holy Scripture tells us that "the eyes of the Lord run to and fro throughout the whole earth, to shew himself strong in the behalf of them whose heart is perfect toward him" (2 Chron. 16:9). As He looked up and down the earth in search of such a man to put upon the throne of Israel, He saw a faithful shepherd lad who answered the description. David was not perfect, but his heart was perfect toward God; that is, he had put himself in a right relationship to God, and God had shown Himself strong toward him even while he was a boy tending his father's sheep.

When a lion and a bear tried to carry off a lamb, David rushed upon them and killed them in the strength of God. In delivering the lamb, his thought was not for himself but for his father's sheep. The people of Israel were the Lord's sheep, and God wanted just such a faithful, loving, unselfish shepherd to place over them. God wanted someone who would recognize the kingly office as that of a shepherd and feel himself responsible to protect the Lord's flock from the lions and bears that surrounded them. (The name *David* probably meant "leader.")

From chapter 16 to the end of the book, covering a period of about fifteen years, Saul and David are the main characters. As has been shown in earlier lessons, the record of Saul is one of continuous decline, culminating in his death (chap. 31). But in the same passages David manifests from time to time those qualities of courage and faith that would serve him well when he reached the throne (2 Sam. 5).

This lesson concerns the commencement of David's public career: his anointing to be king and his first service in the court of Saul.

I. ANALYSIS

The paragraph divisions to be observed for this section are at 16:1, 4, 14; 17:1, 12, 17, 26, 32, 41, 55.

After you have completed your studies in connection with the first readings of these two chapters, make a topical study of the place of the Lord in the narrative. You will find many inspiring insights in this passage. Use the accompanying work sheet to record your studies. Suggested headings are furnished.

Consider these questions in your studies:

1. Did Eliab fail to qualify as king because of his attractive countenance and imposing stature (16:6-7)?

____

Did David qualify because of his handsome appearance (16:12)?

____

What was God's requirement?

____

____

2. Identify: "Spirit *of* the Lord" and "evil spirit *from* the Lord" (16:14).

____

____

Why did God send the latter?

____

CHOSEN of the LORD	**16:1-3**
EYES of the LORD	**16:4-13**
SPIRIT of the LORD	**16:14-23**
ENEMY of the LORD	**17:1-25**
CAUSE of the LORD	**17:26-31**
HELP of the LORD	**17:32-40**
NAME of the LORD	**17:41-54**
THE LORD'S ANOINTED	**17:55-58**

Does He do this today?

3. See 17:1-11. What was Goliath's arrogant challenge?

Compare this with the spirit of Jesus' enemies at the time of the crucifixion.

Read 1 Peter 5:8 for a description of the devil's opposition to the saints.
4. What noble quality of David's heart do you see in 17:26?

5. What evidences of David's faith are in these chapters? List some important lessons about faith to be learned from this.

6. Study the Christian's armor of Ephesians 6.
7. State some of the ways in which David typifies Christ in the narratives of these chapters.

II. COMMENTS

A. David Anointed King

Christ is the true King and Shepherd of His people, and in David we have this greater King foreshadowed in many instances. Observe that even in the first lines of David's biography there appears a correspondence between the lives of Jesus and David: both were from Bethlehem (cf. 16:4).

While Samuel was mourning because Israel's king had failed and had been set aside, God sent him to Bethlehem to anoint David for that office. Samuel's hesitation and fear of Saul (16:2) was natural but nevertheless regretful. God reminded Samuel of the nature of the ceremony of anointing a king for Israel. This was not to be merely a political act; it involved God and was connected with sacrifice.

Notice from 16:13 that the Spirit came upon David at the beginning of his career, as the Spirit descended upon Christ before He began His ministry.

At King Saul's request, David was taken from his father's home to serve Saul as his armor-bearer. He also served the king in playing the harp to drive out evil spirits from Saul. David, though anointed king of Israel, did not hesitate to take his place as a servant, even as his great antitype, Christ, though in the form of God, "made himself of no reputation, and took upon him the form of a servant" (Phil. 2:7).

B. David and Goliath

This story is familiar to Christians; nevertheless it should be carefully read and deeply pondered. It not only illustrates how any child of God, going forth clothed in the strength of the Lord, can overcome evil; it also presents a picture of the great conflict that took place when Jesus met and conquered Satan. Some of the details exhibit startling similarities.

Christ, like David, was sent from His Father's home to look after the welfare of His brethren and to bring them gifts. He also saw Satan's hosts drawn up in battle array against trembling humanity. He was their anointed King, though unrecognized at that time. He was ready to meet in single combat the dreadful foe of the human race. He was misunderstood and despised by His brethren. He met and overcame Satan not by the use of carnal weapons but by the Word of God and in the power of His Spirit. And by so doing, He not only broke the power of the enemy and glorified God, but He has inspired His brethren—God's children—with faith and courage that enable them to put their enemies to flight.

If we but enter into this story of David and Goliath and realize that it is "written for our learning," surely it cannot fail to inspire us. Truly the "whole armour of God" (Eph. 6:13-17) enables us to stand against the wiles of the devil.

III. SUMMARY

As a summary exercise, scan these chapters and list the prominent traits of David that fitted him to be God's candidate for king of Israel.

Lesson 8 — *1 Samuel 18:1–21:9*

David Flees Saul

The setting of the remainder of 1 Samuel is essentially one of the estrangement of a bad king in office from a good king waiting to serve in God's time.

One might legitimately ask why God waited so long to remove Saul and enthrone David. The answer is not one but multifold, as suggested in the following purposes of God:

1. *Judgment.* The woes of judgment for sin are not fleeting. Saul and Israel were to reap years, not just days, of judgment.

2. *Training and preparation.* David was to learn by experience some of the strong disciplines needed for a successful term of leadership. (Read 20:22.) Also, the people themselves needed to be prepared for the next monarch.

3. *Exposure.* Every page of the narrative exposes the exceeding wretchedness of sin and, in bright contrast, the glory of righteousness. We today must see this on the printed page, even as God wanted His people of that day to witness it in person.

The chapters of this lesson mainly concern Saul's attempts at David's life. But David was not without personal friends, of whom Jonathan was the dearest. And so the tone of the narrative is really dual: love (of friends) and hate (of an enemy).

I. ANALYSIS

You are encouraged to analyze this passage by an approach and method of your own choosing. Be sure to read the text carefully, recording your observations generously. The accompanying work sheet suggests an outline and also provides space for some observations.

DAVID FLEES FROM SAUL
1 SAMUEL 18:1—21:9

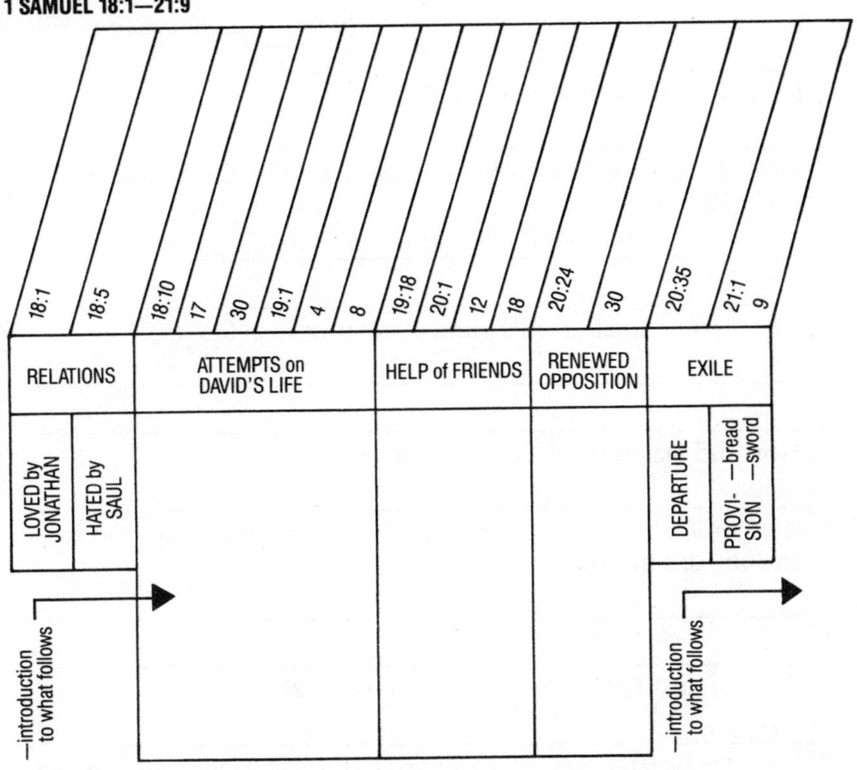

1. How do the first two paragraphs introduce what follows?

____

____

2. What was the cause of Saul's enmity against David? (Cf. 18:8, 12 and other verses.)

____

____

____

3. Why might Jonathan have been jealous of David?

____

____

____

What were some qualities of the love between these two men?

What place did each give to the Lord?

4. How do you account for Saul's temporary change of heart (19:4-7)? (Cf. 19:8-9.)

How do you explain Saul's joining the prophets (19:23)?

5. How did David react to Saul's hatred?

Did he quit serving the people? Did he seek vengeance? On what occasions did he sin?

6. Can you justify David's description of 21:2?

7. How are bread (21:3) and a sword (21:9) symbolic of that which the Christian needs to live by?

8. What does this passage teach about jealousy, love, opposition, trust, success, and the folly of fighting God's anointed?

II. COMMENTS

Jonathan's attitude toward David is indicative of the attitude of the redeemed soul that must please Christ most. Read 18:4. No doubt Jonathan appreciated the value of the *work* of David as much as did his fellowmen. But he was so delighted with the *person* of David that his heart just overflowed with love and he wanted to give David everything he had. It is when we come to love Christ for Himself and what He *is*, rather than for what He *does*, that we are ready to strip ourselves and hand everything we have over to Him. Jonathan did not have much to give besides his love, but surely David valued it far more than the military position that Saul gave him (18:5).

Saul's early favor of David did not come from love; hence it was of short duration. When the women sang their song of 18:6-7 to the returning soldiers, that word "ten" fell upon Saul's ears and awoke the demon of jealousy within him. It is as though they had said, "Saul has done a great work, but David a greater." Saul could not bear to be second. "And Saul eyed David from that day and forward" (18:9). Christian workers need to watch lest they fall to the temptation that overcame Saul—that of jealousy of another whom God has used more mightily.

From then on Saul was determined to kill David, even though he knew perfectly well that he was going against God's purposes. He knew God had chosen David to succeed him (20:30-31), and he knew that the Lord was with David (18:28). Notwithstanding, "Saul became David's enemy continually," thus deliberately determining to thwart God's purposes.

But Saul might as well have hoped to stop the sun in its course as to end David's life until God's time came. A "hedge" (Job 1:10) is set around God's children, and nothing can touch them unless God permits.

Jonathan's firm belief that David would be king (20:14-17), coupled with his unfaltering loyalty to his friend, showed how ineffective in his heart was the poison that had taken control of Saul's heart. Jonathan was a deeply religious man and recognized God's dealings in this matter. So free was he from jealous ambition that he could ardently love the one who would take the throne, which—humanly speaking—belonged to him by right of inheritance.

As a man and a friend, Jonathan was greatly to be admired. As a man he was strong and dexterous with his bow, fearless in battle, never afraid to speak the truth, generous, affectionate, tender as a woman. Above all, he trusted and obeyed God. As a friend he proved himself worthy of the name. Not only did Jonathan avow his friendship when David's victory over Goliath caused him to be admired by all Israel, but his love and friendship burned just as brightly when David was in disfavor at court, hunted, persecuted, hidden, and unacknowledged. Jonathan was not afraid or ashamed to own David and to speak for him among his enemies. It was with confidence, therefore, that he asked to be remembered in the future when David would be the acknowledged king with all power in the land.

Every one of us should show such friendship toward Christ, remembering His words: "Whosoever therefore shall confess me before men, him will I confess also before my Father which is in heaven. But whosoever shall deny me before men, him will I also deny before my Father which is in heaven" (Matt. 10:32-33). A time is coming when we shall be glad to have Him confess us. So while He is unpopular, unacknowledged, and hidden, let us not be ashamed or afraid to confess Him before men.

III. SUMMARY

In these chapters is related the story of a *hero of Israel,*
LOVED by a son of the king,
ACCEPTED by the subjects of the king,
who becomes a *fugitive from Israel* because he is
HATED by the king himself.

Lesson 9

1 Samuel 21:10–28:2

David in Exile

In the last lesson David miraculously escaped Saul's sword in murderous plots that took place in the homeland. The story of this lesson presents David the refugee, spending many months in *real* exile in the foreign land of Philistia and spending more months in *virtual* exile in the barren wilderness of southern Judah. During the latter time Saul renewed his pursuit of David, and as a consequence the two men experienced some heart-searching encounters.

Because there are many chapters in this lesson, you may want to study the entire section in more than one study unit. The survey given later in this lesson will suggest individual units for such studies.

Of necessity only the highlights of these chapters can be touched upon in this one lesson. For help in the geography of the lesson, consult a commentary or Bible dictionary. Have fixed in your mind the two *general* areas of activity of these chapters: Philistia, the southwestern coastal region, and the wilderness of Judah, the mountainous region just west of the Dead Sea where David kept fleeing the pursuing Saul.

I. ANALYSIS

First, read through the entire passage, noting your major impressions and observing key words and phrases as well as other prominent items.

One of your observations will center on the *variety* of David's experiences during these years of exile. It will help you to see the many individual parts of this narrative compiled in groups. Since the accompanying diagram serves this purpose, study it carefully, marking the divisions and outlines in your Bible. This return to the Bible text and read the story a second time with this survey in mind.

1 SAMUEL 21:10—28:3

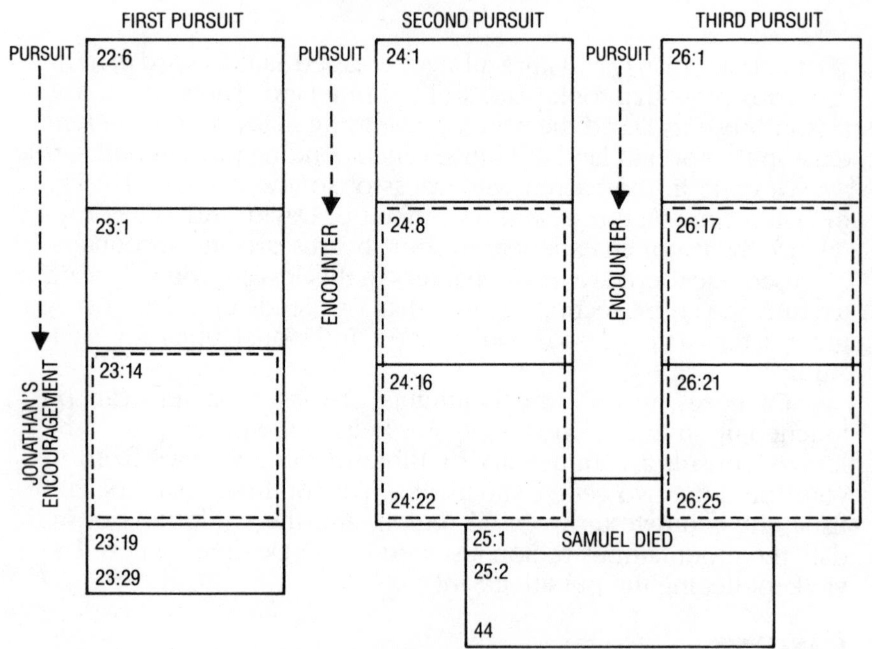

21:10-15
DAVID SEEKS REFUGE in PHILISTIA
—ACHISH REJECTS DAVID—
22:1-5
DAVID in EXILE
(NO REFUGE in PHILISTIA or JUDAH)
DAVID RETURNS to JUDAH (22:5)
PURSUIT by SAUL RENEWED (22:6)
FIRST PURSUIT
SECOND PURSUIT
THIRD PURSUIT
PURSUIT
22:6
23:1
JONATHAN'S ENCOURAGEMENT
23:14
23:19
23:29
PURSUIT
24:1
ENCOUNTER
24:8
24:16
24:22
PURSUIT
26:1
ENCOUNTER
26:17
26:21
26:25
25:1
SAMUEL DIED
25:2
44
LAPSE of DAVID; RETURN to PHILISTIA
27:1
DAVID GIVEN REFUGE in PHILISTIA
27:7
DAVID SERVES ACHISH
28:2

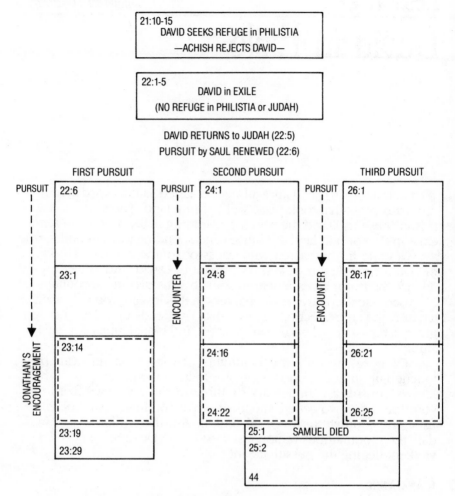

Record observations in the appropriate boxes on the accompanying diagram. (For more space to record, copy the format of the diagram onto large pieces of paper).

Three key passages of this section are shown on the diagram. They are: 23:14-18; 24:8-22; 26:17-25. You may choose to analyze these separately on an analytical chart.

1. Compare the beginning (21:10-15) and end (27:1–28:2) of this story, as shown on the diagram.

2. Notice how each of the three pursuits by Saul brought on vindication for David.

3. Chapter 25 is parenthetical only in the sense that Saul is not part of its action. Chronologically, it is correctly located between chapters 24 and 26.

4. See 21:10-15. Identify two sins of David here.

____

____

5. See 22:1-5. Notice that David wanted to know God's will for him at this time. What was it?

____

____

Did David obey?

____

____

On the prophet Gad, see 2 Samuel 24:11; 1 Chronicles 29:29; 2 Chronicles 29:25.

6. See 22:6-23. In what sense had David "occasioned" the slaughter of the priests of Nob?

____

____

How does this illustrate the principle of reaping for sin?

____

____

7. See 23:14-18. David was in need of two things: victory and encouragement. How was he given each?

____

____

8. See 23:18-29. Read Psalm 54 (including its title) for insight into David's feelings during the threat from the Ziphim (23:20).

9. See 24:8-15. Analyze David's appeal. What did he claim?

Of what did he warn?

10. See 24:16-22. Analyze Saul's response. Was Saul justified in his request of verse 21?

11. See chapter 25. Explain such a brief mention of Samuel's death (v. 1) in view of all that was written of him earlier in the book.

David's request of verse 8 was fair and in accordance with the customs of the land. What was his sin in verse 13?

Is any other sin of David recorded in this chapter?

12. See 26:1-16. Why did David spare Saul (26:9-11)?

13. See 26:17-20. Analyze David's appeal here and compare it with the earlier one (24:8-15). Observe the four places in this chapter where the phrase "the Lord's anointed" appears. What is suggested by the word "anointed"? (The title *Christ* is derived from a Greek word *chrio* meaning "anoint.")

14. See 26:21-25. Do you sense a note of finality in Saul's words of 26:21, 25?

15. See 27:1-6. What was David's sin here?

Comment on 27:1*b* ("There is nothing better for me than . . .").

16. See 27:7–28:2. Notice Achish's words: "He shall be my servant for ever" (27:12). Compare this with God's will for David.

17. What important lessons did David learn from all his experiences during these exile years?

II. COMMENTS

"And David arose, and fled that day" (21:10). These are indeed strange words to be reading of David, who, until this time, had been a man of remarkable faith and courage. But now he had failed in both. He began by misrepresenting things to Ahimelech (21:1-9); then, out of fear of Saul, he fled to the Philistines, Israel's strongest enemy, and presented himself to Achish, king of Gath.

Thus began a period of exile and flight that brought heart-searching experiences to this man of God. Six chapters later in the narrative David is back again at Gath, fleeing to King Achish for help. David's faith in God was at a low ebb for him to utter such words as those of 27:1. He was running away from God, and it was of the mercy of God that he was not consumed.

The Ziklag experience of David was dark indeed. Throughout it all we do not once hear him mention God. Not once is there a song on his lips. Not once do we hear of the priest or the prophet or David consulting with God. Let each child of God take solemn warning. When clouds gather around, and faith begins to weaken, let us not in sudden panic "speedily escape into the land of the Philistines," but rigidly and persistently continue to trust in the Lord with all our heart and wait patiently for Him.

III. SUMMARY

The following outline summarizes in a general way the four refugee situations experienced by David in the story of these chapters:

1. David seeks refuge in Philistia but is not received (21:10-15).

2. David, as a man without a country, finds no refuge in Philistia or Judah (22:1-5).

3. David returns to Judah, dwelling under cover in the caves of the wilderness as he is pursued by Saul (22:6–26:25).

4. David seeks refuge again in Philistia; this time he is received (27:1–28:2).

Lesson 10

1 Samuel 28:3–31:13

Last Days of Saul's Reign

In these chapters is recorded the tragic end of the God-forsaken monarch Saul, who died in battle against an enemy of Israel, the Philistines. David, by divine design, was far from the battle scene when Saul died, being prepared of God to soon sit upon the vacant throne. The last four chapters of 1 Samuel tell a fascinating though tragic story of the last days of Saul's reign.

I. ANALYSIS

From your first reading of these chapters it will not be difficult to sense a continuity in the narrative, even though four different events are involved. The accompanying chart should be used as a work sheet to record key words and phrases.

1. Notice how chapters 28, 29, and 31 are connected by references to the Philistines. Chapter 30 serves as a connecting link, not to any passage in 1 Samuel but to the first chapter of 2 Samuel, where David becomes *the* main character.

2. *See 28:3-25*. What are the indications here that Saul has come to the end of his career?

____

____

When does God refuse to answer man's request?

____

Did Saul actually hear words from Samuel?

____

Was it the woman of Endor or was it the Lord who caused Samuel to speak?

____

1 SAMUEL 28:3—31:13

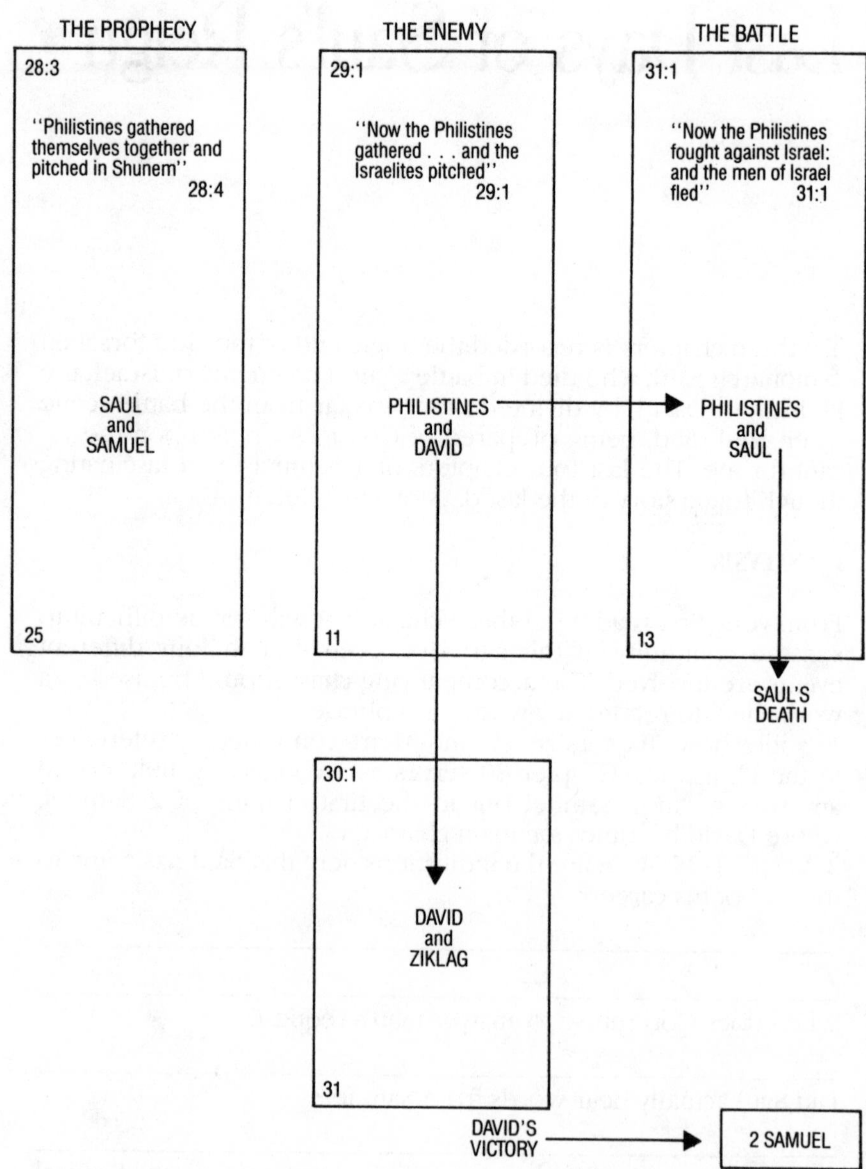
THE PROPHECY
28:3
"Philistines gathered themselves together and pitched in Shunem"
28:4
SAUL
and
SAMUEL
25
THE ENEMY
29:1
"Now the Philistines gathered . . . and the Israelites pitched"
29:1
PHILISTINES
and
DAVID
11
THE BATTLE
31:1
"Now the Philistines fought against Israel: and the men of Israel fled"
31:1
PHILISTINES
and
SAUL
13
SAUL'S
DEATH
30:1
DAVID
and
ZIKLAG
31
DAVID'S
VICTORY
2 SAMUEL

3. *Chapter 29*. How were the Philistine princes wiser than their king, Achish?

How do you suppose this experience of David could have helped him spiritually?

Account for his words of treason in verse 8.

4. *Chapter 30*. What good qualities of David are seen here?

Explain the Lord's blessing on him in view of the events that immediately preceded.

5. *Chapter 31*. How is this chapter a commentary on the total career of Saul?

What are your thoughts concerning Jonathan's being slain by the Philistines in the same battle?

II. COMMENTS

A. Saul's Last Crisis

The Philistines, the most formidable and persevering of Israel's enemies, had again assembled for war. This time their numbers were so vast that Saul feared defeat. In this last crisis of his life he felt his need of God. But it was too late; God would not answer. It would not have been too late for Saul to humble himself before God, confess his sin, and surrender his heart. But his stubborn self-will continued to the end. He wanted God's help, but he wanted it on his own terms. When he received no answer from God, he did not search to find in himself the cause for the silence and put himself in right relationship with God so that He could answer. Instead he immediately did something that God had emphatically forbidden and that Saul himself had ruled against—he consulted a woman engaged in the practice of witchcraft. He was so determined to have his own way and know the future that he dared to disregard God's solemn warnings against occultism.

B. Saul and the Spirit of Samuel

At Saul's request, Samuel's spirit was brought back from sheol, the abode of the spirits of all the dead of Old Testament days. It is evident that God accomplished this feat, not the woman. "The more modern orthodox commentators are almost unanimous in the opinion that the departed prophet did really appear and announce the coming destruction of Saul and his army. They hold, however, that Samuel was brought up not by the magical arts of the witch, but through a miracle wrought by the omnipotence of God."[1]

One might ask, Is it possible to communicate with the dead in these days? Resorting to such communications, when God is not a part, is traffickng in the world of demons. James Gray once wrote, "These demons may sometimes impersonate the dead, deceiving the mediums as well as their clients, it may be, and furnishing another argument why we should have nothing to do with them; but they are not the dead whom we knew and loved, and never can be." All attempts at spirit communication are decidedly wrong because God positively forbids and condemns it. Read Leviticus 19:31; 20:6, 27; Deuteronomy 18:9-12; Isaiah 8:19-20; 1 Timothy 4:1; Revelation 21:8; 1 Chronicles 10:13.

C. David and the Philistines

When the Philistines were gathering to fight Israel, David, who had not left King Achish, was in a deplorably backslidden condition. He was actually marching toward Aphek at the rear of the Philistine army, which was on its way to fight against the chosen people of God. We cannot believe that David relished this position. Jonathan, his beloved friend, was to engage in the coming battle; "the Lord's anointed" (Saul) was to lead the Israelites; and the people whom David was opposing were *God's* people. But David had got himself into such a web of deception in the court of the trustful King Achish, who had absolute confidence in him, that

1. Charles F. Pfeiffer and Everett F. Harrison, eds., *The Wycliffe Bible Commentary* (Chicago: Moody, 1962), p. 292.

the only course open seemed to be to agree to the proposition and go with Achish. It was only because of the Philistine lords' insistence that David was relieved of the predicament and sent away.

D. David and Ziklag

The chastening hand now rested heavily upon this erring, backslidden man. Through affliction, loss, and sorrow God spoke to the heart of David. On his return to Ziklag he found that during his absence the Amalekites had come to the town, burned it, and carried away captive the women and children. Awful as the blow was to his people, David had the hardest burden to bear. At this moment the love and loyalty of his men turned to sudden hatred, and they talked of stoning him. Perhaps this was because he had not left more soldiers behind to defend the town when he started to war with Achish.

Doubtless this overwhelming trouble was allowed to come upon David to drive him back to God. And this is the effect that it had. As he stood there amid the ruins of his home, deserted by his men, his thoughts turned back to the One who had never forsaken him, and we read, "But David encouraged himself in the Lord his God. And David said to Abiathar the priest, . . . I pray thee, bring me hither the ephod . . . And David inquired of the Lord, . . . And He answered him" (30:6-8). How ready the backsliding child of God should be to welcome chastisement if God can bring him to repentance by this means.

E. Saul's Death

The Philistines engaged the Israelites in battle on Mount Gilboa, located south of the eastern part of the Plain of Jezreel. God was not with Israel. They were scattered and slain. Saul's sons, including Jonathan, were slain, and Saul himself was fatally wounded by the arrows of the enemy archers. In his dying moments he besought his armor-bearer to kill him; when the man refused to do so, Saul "took a sword, and fell upon it." This is the first suicide recorded in the Bible.

Thus a career, which at the outset had promised to be one of the brightest in history, ended in thick darkness. It might not have been so except for the fact that Saul insisted on his own way rather than God's. See the comment on Saul's death in 1 Chronicles 10:13.

III. SUMMARY

As a summary exercise, tell the story of these chapters, using the following quotations in the course of your narrative:

"The Lord answered him not"
"God is departed from me"
"The Lord hath rent the kingdom out of thine hand"
"What do these Hebrews here?"
"Nevertheless the lords favor thee not"
"David encouraged himself in the Lord his God"
"Tarrieth by the stuff"
"So Saul died"

Lesson 11

2 Samuel 1:1-27

Background and Survey

The second book of Samuel picks up the story concerning the death of Saul from the last chapter of 1 Samuel. In this lesson we will study David's lament for Saul and Jonathan, as 2 Samuel 1 records it. However, before considering that chapter, we will follow our study pattern by first considering the background of 2 Samuel and then viewing the book as a whole.

I. BACKGROUND

Such items as authorship, date written, and place in the canon have already been discussed in Lesson 1. Most of what applies to 1 Samuel applies as well to 2 Samuel. You would do well to review that lesson at this time.

Now we will consider those things that pertain uniquely to 2 Samuel.

A. Purposes of 2 Samuel

This book has at least two main purposes in its writing:

1. *To record some highlights of David's reign.* Of course this history book does not pretend to be comprehensive. The authors, with the guidance of the Holy Spirit, selected those events from this period of David's life that would serve to impart the message God intended for the reader. Some events not recorded here, but occurring about the same time, are found in other books, such as 1 Chronicles. (The Bible portions describing David's life are 1 Sam. 16–1 Kings 2:11; 1 Chron. 11–29; and many psalms. There are fifty-eight New Testament references to David. For study on

the biography of David, consult a harmony of these books by William Day Crockett.)[1]

For orientation in your study of 2 Samuel, keep the accompanying simple chart in mind.

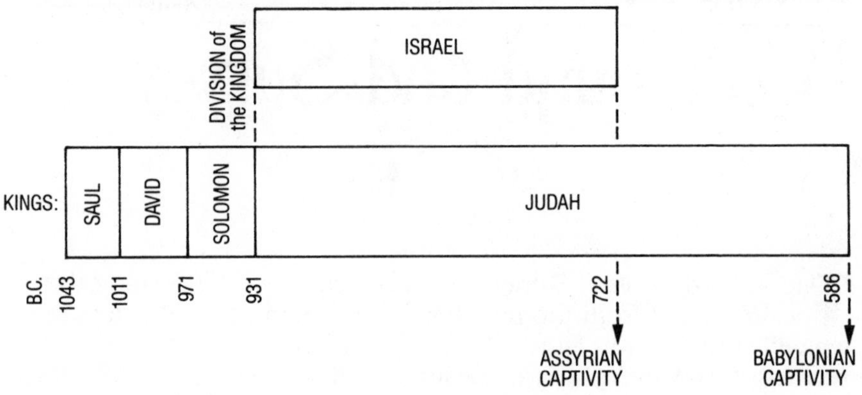

Observe that David's reign lasted forty years. Read 2 Samuel 5:4-5.

Of the many ingredients of this narrative of 2 Samuel, four are given prominence:

a king	David	e.g., 2:4
a city	Jerusalem	5:6-12
	Zion	5:7; 6:1-17
a covenant	Davidic	7:8-17
a kingdom	everlasting	7:16; 23:1-7

2. *To teach important spiritual truths.* Among the truths that you will be observing as you proceed in your study are those about God and His relationship to the believer. Much may be learned of the will of God, the help of God, dependence on God and rewards of God. For a preliminary study on the believer's *dependence on God*, read these verses: 2:1; 5:3; 6:16, 21; 7:18; 8:6, 14; 12:16; 22:1. The book also teaches much about sin and its workings, punishment, and pardon.

Determine to learn all that God wants to teach you in this book and then walk in the light of those truths.

1. *A Harmony of the Books of Samuel, Kings and Chronicles* (Grand Rapids: Baker, 1954).

B. A Title and Key Verse

Since this book relates the highlights of David's career as king of Israel, an appropriate title is THE SECOND KING OF ISRAEL, DAVID. In line with this, a key verse is 5:4.

C. The Man David

David son of Jesse was a man after God's heart and in a life-span of some seventy years "served his own generation by the will of God" (Acts 13:36). David "stood out as a bright and shining light for the God of Israel. His accomplishments were many and varied; man of action, poet, tender lover, generous foe, stern dispenser of justice, loyal friend, he was all that men find wholesome and admirable in man, and this by the will of God, who made him and shaped him for his destiny."[2]

David was not perfect, and the recording of his sins in the Bible should serve as a warning to us to guard against the subtle temptations of Satan. Included is a comparative study of the two controls in David's life.[3]

WHEN GOD'S SPIRIT WAS IN CONTROL	WHEN SELFISH DESIRES WERE IN CONTROL
He had men's devotion (1 Chron. 12:18) and women's (1 Sam. 19:12-13)	He failed to restrain Joab (2 Sam. 3:39) and his own family (2 Sam. 13:21)
He cared for the helpless (2 Sam. 9:1)	He was brutal with captives (2 Sam. 8:2)
He confessed his own sins (Ps. 51) and his enemies' nobility (2 Sam. 1:23)	He would not admit error (2 Sam. 19:29) and repudiated former pardons (1 Kings 2:8)
His piety was shameless (2 Sam. 6:21)	He practiced deception (1 Sam. 21:2)
His faith was radiant (Ps. 23)	His sin was heinous (2 Sam. 11)

Though David's career was marred by sin, he was honest and contrite enough to acknowledge his sins and seek God's forgiveness. No man in the Bible gives a more instructive example of confession than David.

2. J. D. Douglas, ed., *The New Bible Dictionary* (Grand Rapids: Eerdmans, 1962), p. 296.
3. J. Barton Payne, *An Outline of Hebrew History* (Grand Rapids: Baker, 1954), p. 110.

After you have completed your study of 2 Samuel, you will want to compose your own description of David on the basis of both books of Samuel.

II. SURVEY

Review the procedures of study used in survey, as outlined in Lesson 1. Then proceed to make a survey of 2 Samuel, following those procedures. Refer to the accompanying chart only after you have completed your own study.

The main point to observe in this chart is the *pivotal point* of 2 Samuel. That point is at chapters 11 and 12: DAVID'S SIN. Before this, David enjoyed triumphs. After this, even though he confessed his sin and was pardoned, David reaped sin's recompense in various troubles. This simple outline faithfully represents the main flow of the narrative. Refer to it often in your Christian ministry as an illustration of the eternal law of returns, "Whatsoever a man soweth, that shall he also reap" (Gal. 6:7).

III. ANALYSIS OF 2 SAMUEL 1

This chapter serves as a transitional chapter, connecting 1 Samuel 31 (Saul's death) and 2 Samuel 2 and following (David on the throne). It is an appropriate introduction to 2 Samuel, for it reveals the tenderness of the heart of David, a quality that appears again and again throughout the book.

The chapter may be divided into three parts: Report (1-10); Reaction (11-16); Lament (17-27). Devote most of your analysis to the last two paragraphs.

1. What is the main subject of this chapter?

___

Who is the main actor?

___

2. Identify an atmosphere for each of the three paragraphs.

___

___

___

3. See 1:1-10. Compare this report with the record of 1 Samuel 31:1-7. What part of the report was false? (Cf. 4:10.)

___

2 SAMUEL THE SECOND KING of ISRAEL, DAVID

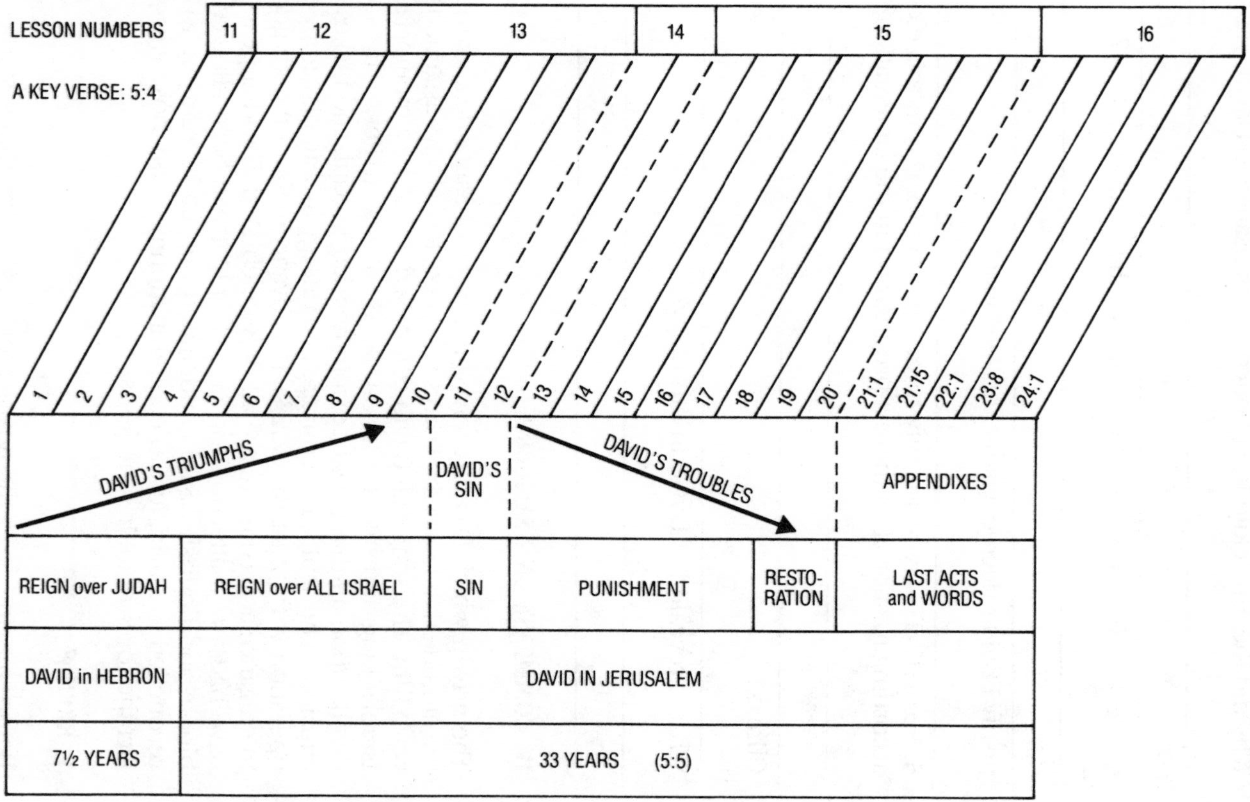

LESSON NUMBERS: 11 (ch. 1–2), 12 (ch. 3–5), 13 (ch. 6–11), 14 (ch. 12–13), 15 (ch. 14–21:1), 16 (ch. 21:15–24)

A KEY VERSE: 5:4

Chapters: 1, 2, 3, 4, 5, 6, 7, 8, 9, 10, 11, 12, 13, 14, 15, 16, 17, 18, 19, 20, 21:1, 21:15, 22:1, 23:8, 24:1

1–9		10–12	12–20		21:1–24
DAVID'S TRIUMPHS		DAVID'S SIN	DAVID'S TROUBLES		APPENDIXES
REIGN over JUDAH	REIGN over ALL ISRAEL	SIN	PUNISHMENT	RESTORATION	LAST ACTS and WORDS
DAVID in HEBRON	DAVID IN JERUSALEM				
7½ YEARS	33 YEARS (5:5)				

Why did the Amalekite lie? (Notice his obeisance to David, 1:2.)

____

____

4. See 1:11-16. Who were the objects of the mourning? (v. 12).

____

____

Justify David's decree against the Amalekite.

____

5. See 1:17-27. Try to identify three different stanzas in this elegy, according to subject. Is there a progression in the lamentation?

____

____

Climax?

____

What is revealed of David in this elegy?

____

____

IV. COMMENTS ON 2 SAMUEL 1

The way in which David received the news of Saul's death reveals the attitude that he, as the Lord's anointed, had always assumed toward him. The song that David composed was to be a memorial of Israel's king and his eldest son. W. G. Blaikie writes, "The song dwells upon all that could be commended in Saul, and makes no allusion to his faults. His courage and energy in war, his happy cooperation with Jonathan (v. 23), his advancement of the kingdom in elegance and comfort, are all duly celebrated. David appears to have had a real affection for Saul, if only it had been allowed to bloom and flourish." Saul condemned himself by refusing to be reconciled to David, just as condemnation rests on those who reject the lover of their soul, Jesus.

V. REVIEW

Before moving on to the next lesson, review the things studied in this exercise. Throughout your study of 2 Samuel try to retain the outline of the survey chart in your mind.

Lesson 12 *2 Samuel 2:1–4:12*

David's Reign over Judah

King Saul was dead, and David knew that he had been anointed by the Lord to rise to the throne at this hour. One would expect that his accession would have been without incident or challenge. But it was not. Opposition dies hard, as David had learned during his years as a fugitive. The chapters of this lesson describe the bloodstrewn pathway to the throne of Israel.

I. ANALYSIS

Read the three chapters carefully and become acquainted with the main characters. The accompanying work sheet can serve as a place for you to record your observations. Let your study be centered on the key verse, 3:1.

1. See 2:1-4*a*. Observe how specific David was in his inquiries of God. What does this teach about prayer and the will of God?

2. See 2:4*b*-7. Observe the three different types of kindness mentioned in verses 5 and 6. What was David's purpose in sending the message to the men of Jabesh-gilead?

Was David being hypocritical in his respect for Saul?

3. See 2:8-11. Who made Ishbosheth king over all Israel?

2 SAMUEL 2-4

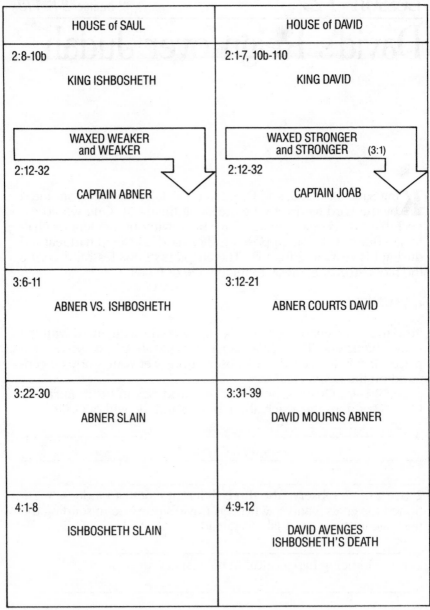

HOUSE of SAUL	HOUSE of DAVID
2:8-10b KING ISHBOSHETH WAXED WEAKER and WEAKER 2:12-32 CAPTAIN ABNER	2:1-7, 10b-110 KING DAVID WAXED STRONGER and STRONGER (3:1) 2:12-32 CAPTAIN JOAB
3:6-11 ABNER VS. ISHBOSHETH	3:12-21 ABNER COURTS DAVID
3:22-30 ABNER SLAIN	3:31-39 DAVID MOURNS ABNER
4:1-8 ISHBOSHETH SLAIN	4:9-12 DAVID AVENGES ISHBOSHETH'S DEATH

Recall the part he played in 1 Samuel.

4. See 2:12-32. Tally the results of the various encounters and battles of these verses. Add to this the note of 3:1. Do you see the hand of God in all of this?

5. See 3:2-5. Three of these sons later turned out to be bitter disappointments to David: Amnon (chap. 13); Absalom (chaps. 13-18); and Adonijah (1 Kings 1:5; 2:25). Suggest possible reasons for this.

6. See 3:12-21. Account for Abner's courting David's favor.

7. See 3:22-39. Observe how the text emphasizes the sincerity of David's lament over Abner's death. How did David's reaction bring him into favor with Israel?

8. Chapter 4. How did the events of this chapter finalize Israel's acceptance of David as king?

9. List some spiritual lessons taught by these chapters on subjects such as patience, love, and dependence on God.

II. COMMENTS

1. Hebron was a fitting place for David to be crowned. It was the oldest city in the land, and here Abraham, Isaac, Jacob, and Joseph, the first four great men of the nation, were buried.

2. The death of Saul did not immediately clear the way to the throne for David. The tribe of Judah, David's own tribe, had acknowledged him as king, but the majority of the people of Israel had not. Crafty Abner capitalized on this.

3. Abner never had any love for David; moreover, he wanted to retain his own position as captain. Joab was already David's trusted commander; in case David became king of the land, Abner felt that his chances for military position would be slender. On the other hand, if Ishbosheth, Saul's son, could be kept on the throne, Abner would have even greater power than he had under Saul because Ishbosheth was a mere figurehead, a weakling whom Abner could control.

4. David's polygamy violated God's instructions regarding kings of Israel (read Deut. 17:17). This sin contributed to David's growing insensitivity to God's moral standards, contributing at least in part to his heinous sin with Bathsheba (chap. 11).

5. Abner's changeover to the side of David can be explained by the fact that Abner began to see that the house of Saul was steadily weakening, while the house of David was increasing in strength. Abner wanted to join the bandwagon of the winners.

6. The strength of David's character at this time is clearly illustrated in his refusal to rejoice over the murders of his enemies Abner and Ishbosheth.

III. SUMMARY

"The war between the houses of Saul and of David was long drawn out; but David became progressively stronger and Saul's house weaker and weaker" (3:1, Berkeley Version).

Lesson 13

2 Samuel 5:1–10:19

David's Reign over All Israel

After reading page after page about the troubles of Israel's first king, Saul, and then about the woes of David, the fugitive, waiting for the throne to be vacated, it is like coming into the glorious sunshine of a bright autumn morning to read that David finally began to reign over all Israel and Judah. In your study of these chapters you will be amply rewarded for diligently applying yourself to see all that God has written here.

Due to limitation of space in this study manual, six full chapters are devoted to just this one lesson. You may choose to make individual studies of some of the chapters. For instance, chapters 6 and 7 are excellent chapters to study in depth by the analytical chart method (with these paragraph divisions: chap. 6, at vv. 1, 6, 12, 16, 20; chap. 7, at vv. 1, 8, 18, 25).

I. ANALYSIS

Follow the usual procedures of analysis, beginning with a careful reading of the text. These chapters describe the bright aspects of David's reign before he marred his record with the sin of chapter 11. Be careful not to anticipate that fall to the extent that the pictures of chapters 5-10 are thereby discolored. Let the natural beauty and the triumphant tone of this passage remain in true character.

Each chapter of this section is a unit by itself, intimately related to the whole. The first five verses of chapter 5 introduce the common subject, for which a title might be "David Begins to Rule over All Israel." The outline on the accompanying work sheet identifies the main subject of each chapter. Use the work sheet to record as many observations as you can. Note especially key words and phrases. Spend much time on chapters 6 and 7.

2 SAMUEL 5-10

5:1	INTRODUCTION		"David . . . began to reign" (5:4)
DAVID'S KINGDOM			
5:6	HEADQUARTERS	CITY HOUSE (THREAT)	
6:1	RELIGION	ARK	
7:1		TEMPLE KINGDOM	
8:1	NATIONAL SECURITY	VICTORIES	
9:1	RELIGION in PRACTICE	KINDNESS at HOME	—kindness accepted
10:1		KINDNESS ABROAD	—kindness rejected

1. *See 5:1-5*. The word translated "feed" (5:2) is the word meaning "to shepherd." (Cf. Jer. 3:15; Ezek. 34.) Compare the tasks of shepherd and captain (5:2).

---

2. *See 5:6-10*. How important was it for Israel to have a capital city?

In what sense was Jerusalem Israel's first capital?

---

3. *Chapter 6*. List some of ten major truths taught here about the Ark of God and its relation to the kingdom.

Read these related passages: Exodus 25:14; Numbers 4:15; 7:9; 1 Chronicles 13:1-8; 15:1-13; 16:1-36. Psalms 15, 24, and 68, three of David's finest psalms, are supposed to have been composed on the occasion of the placing of the Ark in the Tabernacle.
4. Chapter 7. Why did God discourage David from building a house (temple) for Him?

Notice references to the messianic King (e.g., 7:14*a*; cf. Heb. 1:5). What attributes of God are prominent in this chapter?

What good qualities of David are manifested in his prayer of 7:18-29?
(Read 1 Chronicles 17 in connection with this chapter.)

---

5. *Chapter 8.* Observe these key phrases: "David smote"; "the Lord preserved." What spiritual truth is taught here?

---

6. *Chapters 9-10.* Compare these chapters as to kindnesses shown, reactions, and results.

---

7. List ten vital lessons for Christian living taught in these chapters.

II. COMMENTS

A. David's Coronation

The account of David's coronation in 2 Samuel is meager—just three verses (5:1-3). To get an idea of the imposing assembly gathered at Hebron to crown him king over all Israel, read 1 Chronicles 12, beginning with verse 23. By adding the numbers given, we find the size of the assembly totaled about 340,000 armed men, who came from every part of the land; 120,000 of them were from the east of Jordan. They were all "of one heart to make David king." In the speech that they made (2 Sam. 5:1-2) in offering the crown to David, they urged three reasons he should be king over them: first, their relationship to him; second, his past work for them; and third, God's word.

Taking Jerusalem as his capital was one of David's first acts after his coronation. Saul had selected his own city, Gibeah, for his capital, but David selected the city most suitable for the purposes to which it was to be devoted. Moreover, this was the city that God had chosen. Jerusalem was suitable in every way. It was the heart and stronghold of the Canaanites and for hundreds of years had been in their possession. Never in all the years since the days of Joshua had the Hebrews been able to cast out these enemies from

Jerusalem. The Jebusites had such confidence in their fortifications and walls that they laughed at the idea of David's being able to take the city. In derision they boasted that even the blind men and cripples of Jerusalem could defend it against the Hebrew army. "Nevertheless, David took the stronghold of Zion." He dwelt there, defended it against all attempts of the enemy to regain it, and proceeded to make it the political and religious center of the nation. From there he extended his influence until the entire land was under his absolute control.

Thus our blessed Lord can lay hold of the human heart and cast out Satan, no matter how long he may have had possession. The Lord will take up His dwelling place there, defend it against all attempts of the enemy, make it the center of power and worship, and extend His influence further and further until every faculty of our being is under His absolute control and we crown Him Lord of all.

B. The Ark

During Saul's reign the Ark had been almost forgotten. It had remained in the house of Abinadab, who lived at Kirjath-jearim, a few miles from Jerusalem, ever since it was returned from the Philistines many years before. Knowing what place the Ark should have in the religious life of Israel, David recovered it and set it up in the Tabernacle. The sudden death of Uzzah for touching the Ark against God's commandment must have caused the people of Israel and their leaders to diligently search the Scriptures that they had neglected for so long. Sometimes God allows righteous judgment to fall on His creatures in violent ways in this lifetime to cause the hearts of men to turn from their sin and seek His face.

C. The Temple and the Covenant

God refused David's offer to build Him a house, but He spoke His refusal in such a burst of grace and glory and revelation that David forgot to be disappointed and could only marvel at the greatness and goodness of God. It was not that God was displeased with David's desire to build Him a house; indeed, He said, "Thou didst well that it was in thine heart." But God had another plan for His beloved servant. God would build a "house" for *David*. God was reaffirming the covenant that He had originally made with Abraham, a covenant promising an everlasting kingdom, with Christ on its throne.

David wanted to build a temple for God, but Solomon was given the privilege. Undoubtedly the character of David's lifework for God was fighting, not building. But even by fighting he was clearing the way for another to lay the foundation of that house of worship that his heart had so fondly desired to build. After the warring was over, Solomon erected the temple from materials that David had prepared.

David represents Christ in His suffering and victory over the great enemy. Solomon represents Christ in His glory after the suffering and the conflicts are finished. The church, which is the true temple of God, having Christ for its chief cornerstone, will be manifested in the last day. Now in the church's days of suffering and conflict the materials are being prepared for this glorious building of God.

III. SUMMARY

The prospects for Israel at the commencement of David's reign were bright. A central capital city was secured, the symbol of God's presence was restored, the covenant of an everlasting kingdom was renewed, security against enemies was demonstrated, and the loving-kindness of the anointed king was felt at home and abroad. Such were the prospects. The next chapter shows how quickly such splendors can fade.

Lesson 14

2 Samuel 11:1–12:31

David's Sin

David had not reigned long in Jerusalem as king of all Israel before he came to tragic turning point in his career. There had been other times in his history when he left his usual high plane of living and descended into the valley, yielding to such things as unbelief, fear, falsehood, deceit, pride, and anger. But the sins of this day—adultery and murder—were all the more conspicuous because they were committed at the height of his reign.

David was never the same again. As long as he lived, troubles arose to plague him. This outline shows chapters 11 and 12 as the pivotal point in 2 Samuel:

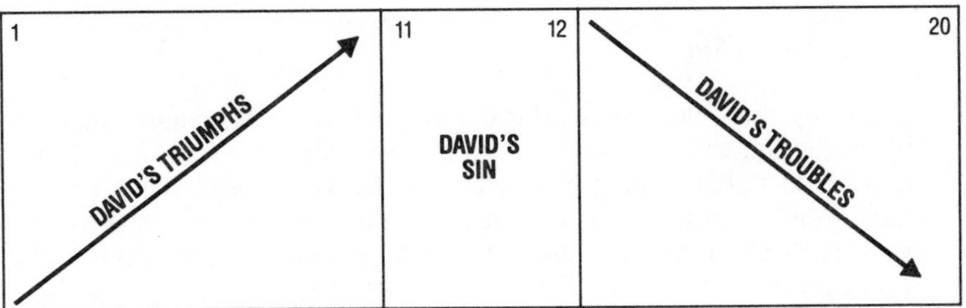

I. ANALYSIS

After reading the two chapters, write down what they teach concerning the following subjects. Add any other subjects that may appear in the course of your study.

A. SIN
1. Environment
2. Temptation
3. The sinner

4. Transgression of the law (Ex. 20:14)
5. Sin begets sin
6. Sin discovered

B. JUDGMENT
1. Judgment inevitable
2. Self-condemnation
3. Divine judgment
4. No respecter of persons
5. Just recompense
6. Soul agony of judgment

C. CONFESSION
1. Personal
2. Explicit
3. Honest
4. Of a broken heart
(Study Ps. 51, which David wrote out of this experience.)
5. Fruits

D. MERCY
1. Forgiveness
2. Atonement (cf. 12:13 with Lev. 20:10)
3. Restored blessing (12:24-25; 26-31)

II. COMMENTS

A. David's Sin

One thing that had prepared the way for David's downfall was his disobedience to God's command against polygamy (Deut. 17:17). Another fact that contributed was that he was not at his post of duty. "And it came to pass, . . . at the time when kings go forth to battle [i.e., in the spring, after the rainy season], . . . David tarried still at Jerusalem" (11:1). David's lifework was that of fighting the Lord's battles; but here we find him idle, off his guard, tarrying in Jerusalem when it was the time for battle. Satan quickly took advantage of that.

It was not only one sin that David committed but a long black chain of sins: idleness, selfishness, covetousness, adultery, deception, treachery, murder—one after the other in quick succession. How little David imagined when that first covetous thought came to him that in a few days he would murder one of his bravest and most loyal soldiers and friends. The depths are untold to which Satan will quickly drag us if once we allow him an edge.

In addition to the direct crimes that David committed, he also gave the enemies of God occasion to blaspheme. He brought great reproach upon the name he bore and the position that he occupied. One can imagine the look on Joab's face when he read the letter that Uriah handed him from David. He might have thought something like this: "Oh, so this psalm-singing king who pretends to be so pious can kill a man treacherously. He made a great to-do when I killed Abner, but it seems to me that putting a good man like Uriah in a place of danger and then deserting him, giving him no chance for his life, is about as contemptible as stabbing a man under the fifth rib for killing one's brother. Besides, I don't pretend to be a saint like my Uncle David. Oh, well, if that is all there is to his religion, I don't want any of it."

The inconsistencies of Christians tend to work havoc in keeping men and women away from the church and God. The Bible that the unsaved read is the lives of professing followers of Christ. They look to Christians to see a sample of what is being offered. Christians are Christ's representatives, and this thought should be a great incentive for us to let nothing in our lives be a stumbling block over which precious souls may fall.

David was temporarily relieved when he learned that Uriah was dead. He would put his sins out of his memory, as things of the past, to be forgotten. Whatever caused David not to see that the Lord knew everything?

"But the thing that David had done displeased the Lord" are the closing words of chapter 11. May no one read this chapter without paying the profoundest regard to these words. In that word "but" lies a world of meaning.

B. David's Repentance

David's sins had so seared his conscience that he did not perceive a picture of his own black deed in Nathan's inspired parable until these words rang through his brain like a pistol shot: "Thou art the man." Then he saw his crime in all its hideousness and realized how just was the sentence that he himself had pronounced upon the sinner.

Each word of the prophet must have cut like a lash into David's sore heart. "I have sinned against the Lord," he cried, condensing into these words all the remorse and anguish and penitence he poured forth in Psalm 51, as he lay prostrate on the earth all night before the Lord. During the days of fasting while Bathsheba's child lay at the point of death, David saw everything in its true light and cried out to God for mercy and pardon and cleansing.

"Against thee, thee only, have I sinned, and done this evil in thy sight" (Ps. 51:4). David saw that his sins against Bathsheba and Uriah were really sins against God.

No sooner had David confessed his sin than God said by the mouth of Nathan, "The Lord also hath put away thy sin" (12:13). A child of God who has fallen into sin need never suppose that he must wait long in praying and agonizing before God will forgive. When one confesses and forsakes his sin, God instantly puts it away. Though consequences may follow, he may know throughout all the trial that he has been forgiven and restored to the Father's favor. Read 1 John 1:9.

III. SUMMARY

The story of these chapters proceeds from broken fellowship to restored fellowship, touching on all the involvements in between:

- TRANSGRESSION
  - DISPLEASURE OF GOD (11:27)
    - EXPOSURE BY GOD (12:7)
    - CONTINUING JUDGMENTS (12:10)
  - CONFESSION (12:13)
- RESTORATION (12:13, 20)

Lesson 15 *2 Samuel 13:1–20:26*

David's Troubles

David's sins against Bathsheba and Uriah were truly forgiven, but the bitter fruits of his sins were invevitable. The death of his week-old child was only the beginning of the storm of judgment that broke upon David's house. This lesson is devoted to the chapters that describe some of the troubles that David experienced in subsequent years.

I. ANALYSIS

Study each chapter with the view to seeing how David was involved in or affected by each trouble. The accompanying work sheet furnishes a general outline of the passage. Use it to record observations.

1. In your first reading, choose chapter titles and record them. Why are segment divisions made at 19:9 and 19:41?

____

____

2. Record the main content of each chapter in a few words.
3. Try making your own outline of this section, comparing it with the one given.
4. Chapter 13. Concerning Amnon, son of David by Ahinoam (3:2), someone has written: "In scripture some men have very short biographies. Amnon is one of these. Like Cain, all that is recorded of him was the mark of infamy." In view of the Mosaic law of Leviticus 18:9, what should have been Amnon's penalty?

____

DAVID'S TROUBLES
2 SAMUEL 13-20

FAMILY TROUBLES		ABSALOM'S REBELLION				DAVID'S RESTORATION	FURTHER STRIFE and REBELLION
13	14	15	16	17	18	19:9	19:41 20:26

Can David's reaction of 13:21 be considered sufficient discipline for the sin of his son?

____

____

Explain David's laxity.

____

____

5. Chapter 14. What were the steps of Absalom's reconciliation with David?

____

____

Why is verse 25 such a striking description of Absalom in view of what the next chapters tell of him?

____

____

6. Chapters 15-18. What do these chapters teach about religion, hate, jealousy, loyalty, love, patience, and perseverance, God's sovereignty, and His righteous judgments?

____

____

____

____

7. See 19:9–20:26. "So the king returned" (19:15). What were the problems of David's return to the throne, and how were they solved?

____

____

____

Compare the speeches of these four men: Joab (10:5-7); Shimei (19:19-20); Mephibosheth (19:26-28, 20); Barzillai (19:34-37).

____

____

____

____

8. What do these chapters reveal of the character of David?

What effects, if any, did his experiences of chapters 11 and 12 have on this part of his life?

II. COMMENTS

In these chapters is described the fulfillment of the prophet Nathan's denunciation and the reaping of the seed that David had sown. Shame, dishonor and murder were committed in David's own family circle. Whereas his own sins had been done in secret, those of his children were before all Israel. David also began to see the fulfillment of God's word that the sword would rise up against him. The prophecies of 12:11-12 came to pass in all their revolting details. In his children's ways, David was brought to understand something of how he had pained his heavenly Father by disobedience and heinous crime. In addition to all this, David had to bear the alienation of his people, the cursing of his subjects, the humiliation of his wives, and the hatred of his son.

A. Absalom's Rebellion

Of all the sons spoken of in the Bible, none was more devoid of natural affection or less sensible to filial duty than this handsome, fascinating prince of Israel. Of Absalom, Matthew Henry writes, "In his body there was no blemish, but in his mind nothing but wounds and bruises."

No sooner was Absalom restored to his former position of favor than he began to plot to get the throne. The first thing he did was to make himself conspicuous by appearing in pomp (15:1). Imagine many in Israel looking upon this handsome young prince with his attendants in glittering uniform and his prancing horses, saying, "This is the kind of a king we should have now that we have become such a great nation, a king that looks the part, not an old man like David riding on a mule, unpretentious, old-fashioned, and far too religious."

Absalom not only attracted attention to his appearance but set about convincing the people of his sympathy and interest in their affairs. He intimated that David was not giving them a fair deal and suggested the improvements that he would make in government if he were king (15:2-5). David had always been a kind, indulgent, loving father who had shown special mercy and favor to this son. Yet Absalom, by flattery, kisses, and fair speech went about deliberately stealing the hearts of the people from the faithful old king, who did not suspect either the treachery of his son or the fickleness of his subjects.

Four years later, under the hypocritical assumption of piety, Absalom obtained his father's permission to go to Hebron. But instead of paying a vow to the Lord, he sent out spies to all the tribes of Israel, ordering them to declare him king in Hebron at the sound of the trumpet. The fickle Israelites quickly gathered around the prince. The conspiracy grew steadily stronger, with some of David's chief men joining the ranks. Among those who followed Absalom was Ahithophel, David's trusted friend and counselor (15:12, 31; 16:15).

But many true hearts in Israel would not desert David in the day of trouble. Many loved him too well to be turned away by Absalom's flatteries. The king's servants proclaimed their readiness "to do whatsoever my lord the king shall appoint." David had nothing to offer his followers save hardship and wandering. But so dear was his person to the faithful ones that each could say with Ittai: "As the Lord liveth, and as my lord the king liveth, surely in what place my lord the king shall be, whether in death or life, even there also will thy servant be" (15:21). How such devotion must have warmed David's stricken heart. He knew now that it was himself they loved and not what he was able to give them.

It is uplifting to observe David's submissive spirit in all the troubles attending him. These he recognized as from the Lord because of his sin. David seemed to feel that no punishment was too great for him, that he deserved even to have the Lord say to him, "I have no delight in thee." And even when Shimei came out cursing and throwing stones, David did not resent it, but said: "Let him alone, and let him curse; for the Lord hath bidden him" (16:11).

It was during this sad period that King David wrote some of his sweetest psalms, among them the third, fourth, sixty-second, and sixty-third. Read the third psalm (noting the title) in connection with his flight from Jerusalem, and you have an insight into David's character—that of trust in God under all circumstances. When we pass through bitter trial, is our confidence as strong in the Lord, and do we make Him the sole Source of our comfort?

Absalom did not occupy the throne at Jerusalem for long. It was not enough that David had fled the city. Absalom could secure the throne only by defeating David in battle. On the day of that battle, Absalom and his army were utterly defeated. Joab, David's captain, showed the young usurper no mercy. Shot through the heart, smitten by the armor-bearers, slain, cast into a pit with stones heaped over his body—that was the fate of the one who had aspired to steal the throne from the God-appointed king of Israel (18:9-17).

When the messengers came running to tell David that the victory was his and that he was again undisputed monarch, the father's heart was not engaged by thoughts of his own glory but with anxiety for his child. "Is the young man Absalom safe?" he cried. He would have given his kingdom and his very life for Absalom. "O my son Absalom, my son, my son Absalom! Would God I had died for thee, O Absalom, my son, my son!" was the heartbroken wail of the king. In every sense of the word he had lost his tenderly beloved son. Any parent who has had like affliction can appreciate something of his suffering. David had won a war and regained a throne, but he had lost his son. Unmindful of all else, he gave himself up to his lament.

B. David's Restoration

Instead of going directly to Jerusalem and taking possession of the capital, David preferred to wait until he had been invited to the throne from which he had been driven. A movement was on foot to enthrone him again, but Judah, David's own tribe, had not joined. Perhaps Judah was afraid because it had been foremost in Absalom's rebellion. Both Hebron, where Absalom was first proclaimed king, and Jerusalem were in the tribe of Judah. But David had resolved upon a policy of clemency. He sent friendly word to Judah to inquire why they had not joined in the national movement to recall him. He reminded them of their close relationship to him and, as if to prove to them that he was willing to forgive and forget the past rebellion, he advanced Amasa, who had been at the head of Absalom's army, to the highest military position. This completely won the hearts of the men of Judah, who sent David a hearty invitation to return and promptly followed the invitation by hurrying to meet him and conduct him back.

But the other tribes had yet to give their full assent, and therein arose another problem. The jealousy of the men of Israel, because they had not been consulted in regard to escorting back the king, caused a quarrel with the men of Judah (19:41-43). This might have been peacefully adjusted if Sheba had not blown the trumpet of sedition at just the critical moment and succeeded in inducing the men of Israel to leave David and follow him. That rebellion was short-lived however, and David was then acknowledged king over all the nation again.

III. SUMMARY

During the years of these chapters David experienced both retribution and restoration from the hand of God. He mourned the death of his sons, saw his people desert him, and fled the throne for his life. But his heart had mellowed much in the last months, so he was prepared to accept the retribution as the disciplining hand of his heavenly Father. Then it was that the Father showed His mighty hand in behalf of David and brought him back to the throne of his divine appointment.

Lesson 16

2 Samuel 21:1–24:25

Appendixes

Apparently the five subjects treated in these chapters are not a chronological continuation of the narrative ending in chapter 20. If such is the case, then each of the units may be studied as an appendix, supplementing the main body of 2 Samuel. (Note: This is not to say that some of the events of 21:1–24:25 did not transpire *after* those of the earlier chapters.)

These chapters of 2 Samuel serve as a fitting conclusion to the book, even though David's last days and his death are not recorded until 1 Kings.

I. ANALYSIS

Study each appendix as a separate unit. The variety of content from unit to unit is typical of appendixes appearing at the close of books.

A. Famine (21:1-14)

Read Ezekiel 14:21 for a list of God's four judgments upon Israel. According to this account of 21:1-14, did God require the price of Saul's sons to appease the Gibeonites?

____

____

What was the purpose of the judgment of famine?

____

B. Philistine Wars (21:15-22)

How does the text reveal that these wars took place toward the end of David's life?

Comment on 21:17*b*.

C. Psalms of Thanksgiving (22:1–23:7)

(The psalm of 23:1-7 is a unit by itself.) Analyze these psalms carefully. Try to identify stanzas (paragraphs) of similar thought. Continue your analysis from that point. List some of the key lines of these psalms. Also recall events in David's life that may have been the setting for some of the lines or stanzas. How fitting is the location of this appendix at the end of the book?

D. David's Mighty Men (23:8-38)

Joab is not cited as one of the heroes. Any explanation?

Comment on the meanings of some of the repeated words of this unit.

E. Census and the Pestilence (24:1-15)

Read 1 Chronicles 21 in connection with this chapter. Note especially the recognition of Satan in 1 Chronicles 21:1. Comparing this with 2 Samuel 24:1, what is taught concerning God's ways?

What was David's sin?

____

____

What does this chapter teach about God's mercies?

____

____

____

What is the key item of 24:18-25?

____

____

How is this a fitting conclusion to 2 Samuel?

____

____

II. COMMENTS

A. The Famine

The lives of the Gibeonites had been secured by an oath that had been made in Joshua's day (Joshua 9:19). Saul broke this oath, although the Bible does not record the events of the violation. Some expositors hold that the famine was all that God intended to bring as judgment for that violation and that the giving over of Saul's sons was judgment for David's sin in inquiring of the Gibeonites rather than of God in regard to what he should do (21:3). Other expositors consider both judgments from God for the one sin, in light of 21:14*b*: "When they had done all that the king commanded, God afterward answered the prayers for the land" (Berkeley Version).

B. Philistine Wars

David began his fighting days with the victory over the giant of Gath, and he ended them with the slaughter, by the hands of his servants, of the giant's four sons (21:15-22).

C. Psalms of Thanksgiving

The imagery is impressive, especially in 21:7-19. It would be difficult to find language anywhere to equal this. Indeed, the song

D. David's Mighty Men

Thirty-seven heroes are honored in this list. The record cites exactly what each one of these mighty men did. Some did less and some did more, but every service is carefully recorded. David's favorites seem to have been the three mentioned in verses 13-17. He refers to them as "the first three" (see vv. 19, 23). This list reminds us of Paul's roll of honor in Romans 16.

The record of our services for our King is kept accurately and will be opened some day. Then we will be rewarded according to our works as soldiers of the cross and workmen in His vineyard.

E. The Census

This last chapter of 2 Samuel is interesting. Notice that numbering the people was considered sinful in the judgment of God, in the judgment of Joab, and finally, in the judgment of David also.

The plague was sent in punishment for David's sin of numbering the people. First Chronicles 21:1 says that Satan moved him to do it, whereas 2 Samuel 24:1 says that God moved him to do it. The two statements can be reconciled by remembering that the Old Testament writers often attribute to God's agency that which He permitted. David was convicted of sin. The sin lay in the motive. David had let pride creep into his heart. He wanted to make a good showing among the nations, and there was a tendency to trust in numbers rather than in God alone. In 24:17 we see his sweet spirit of acknowledging sin and asking to take his punishment himself rather than that others should suffer.

This book closes with David's purchase of the threshing floor on Mt. Moriah, which afterward became the site of the Temple. It was here where hundreds of years earlier Abraham's uplifted hand had been stayed and a ram substituted as a sacrifice in place of Isaac. Not only had the blood of the victim flowed on this spot in Abraham's time, but in David's time the hand of judgment was stayed by mercy and David's sin was blotted out.

A CONCLUDING EXERCISE

Scan the lessons of this manual to recall the highlights of 1 and 2 Samuel. Review the survey charts of both books. Then turn to the book of 1 Chronicles and read the section that describes events of the same period covered by 1 and 2 Samuel. Those chapters are: 1 Chronicles 10-27. Be on the lookout for the familiar and for the new. This should prove to be an interesting project.

Bibliography

RESOURCES FOR FURTHER STUDY

Chain Reference Bible (Thompson). Indianapolis: Kirkbride, 1934.

Crockett, William Day. *A Harmony of the Books of Samuel, Kings, and Chronicles.* Grand Rapids: Baker, 1954.

Deane, W. J. *Samuel and Saul: Their Lives and Times.* Westwood, N.J.: Revell, n.d.

Jensen, Irving L. *Jensen's Survey of the Old Testament.* Chicago: Moody, 1978.

Manley, G. T. *The New Bible Handbook.* Chicago: InterVarsity, 1950.

The New International Version Study Bible. Grand Rapids: Zondervan, 1985.

Pfeiffer, Charles F. *An Outline of Old Testament History.* Chicago: Moody, 1960.

The Ryrie Study Bible. Chicago: Moody, 1978.

Strong, James. *The Exhaustive Concordance of the Bible.* New York: Abingdon, 1890.

Tenney, Merrill C., ed. *The Zondervan Pictorial Bible Dictionary.* Grand Rapids: Zondervan, 1963.

Unger, Merrill F. *The New Unger's Bible Handbook.* Chicago: Moody, 1984.

COMMENTARIES AND TOPICAL STUDIES

Blaikie, William G. *The First Book of Samuel.* London: Hodder and Stoughton, 1898. Also *The Second Book of Samuel*, 1908.

Kiripatrick, A. F. *I, II Samuel.* The Cambridge Bible. Cambridge: Cambridge U., 1930.

Renwich, A. M. "I and II Samuel." In *The New Bible Commentary*, ed. F. Davidson. Grand Rapids: Eerdmans, 1953.

Young, Fred E. "I and II Samuel." In *The Wycliffe Bible Commentary*, ed. Charles F. Pfeiffer and Everett F. Harrison. Chicago: Moody, 1962.

Moody Press, a ministry of the Moody Bible Institute,
is designed for education, evangelization, and edification.
If we may assist you in knowing more about Christ
and the Christian life, please write us without obligation:
Moody Press, c/o MLM, Chicago, Illinois 60610.